The *Acts of Philip*

The *Acts of Philip*
A New Translation

Translated from the Greek by
François Bovon and Christopher R. Matthews

BAYLOR UNIVERSITY PRESS

© 2012 by Baylor University Press
Waco, Texas 76798-7363

All Rights Reserved. No part of this publication may be reproduced, stored in a retrieval system, or transmitted, in any form or by any means, electronic, mechanical, photocopying, recording, or otherwise, without the prior permission in writing of Baylor University Press.

Cover Design by Cindy Dunne, Blue Farm Graphics

Library of Congress Cataloging-in-Publication Data

Acts of Philip. English.
 The acts of Philip : a new translation / translated from the Greek by François Bovon and Christopher R. Matthews.
 122 p. cm.
 Includes bibliographical references (p. 109).
 ISBN 978-1-60258-655-0 (pbk. : alk. paper)
 I. Bovon, François. II. Matthews, Christopher R. III. Title.
 BS2880.P55A3 2012
 229'.925—dc23
                               2012017929

For
Lori Matthews
and
Michelle et Bertrand Bouvier-Bron

CONTENTS

Introduction to the *Acts of Philip*   1

Translation of the *Acts of Philip*   31

Bibliography   109

INTRODUCTION TO THE *ACTS OF PHILIP**

François Bovon

TWENTIETH-CENTURY RESEARCH ON THE *ACTS OF PHILIP*

An essential step in the search for new forms or portions of early Christian apocryphal texts is the consultation of the catalogues of Greek manuscripts.[1] When I was working on the *Acts of Philip* (*APh*), I learned that various parts of that ancient work could be found in Greek hagiographical manuscripts, particularly in the so-called *Menologia* or lives of the saints prepared for their feast days.[2] Since the feast of the apostle

---

* Christopher R. Matthews offered a steadfast contribution and gave important input toward this introduction. He improved the English, suggested needed corrections, and helped me to formulate his own positions, which are sometimes different from mine. I enjoyed this collaboration and express my gratitude to him here.

[1] On the search for new forms or portions of texts, see François Bovon, "Editing the Apocryphal Acts of the Apostles," in *The Apocryphal Acts of the Apostles: Harvard Divinity School Studies* (ed. François Bovon, Ann Graham Brock, and Christopher R. Matthews; Religions of the World; Cambridge, Mass.: Harvard University Center for the Study of World Religions, 1999), 1–35. On using catalogues of Greek manuscripts, see *Répertoire des bibliothèques et des catalogues de manuscrits grecs de Marcel Richard*, rev. Jean-Marie Olivier (3d ed.; CC; Turnhout: Brepols, 1995). See also Albert Ehrhard, *Überlieferung und Bestand der hagiographischen und homiletischen Literatur der griechischen Kirche von den Anfängen bis zum Ende des 16. Jahrhunderts* (3 vols.; TU 50–52; Leipzig: Hinrichs, 1937–1952); and Maurice Geerard, *Clavis Apocryphorum Novi Testamenti* (CC; Turnhout: Brepols, 1992).

[2] A *menologion* is a collection that covers a period of one month, three months, six months, or one year. See J. Noret, "Ménologes, synaxaires, ménées. Essai de clarification," *Analecta Bollandiana* 86 (1968): 21–24.

1

2   The *Acts of Philip*

Philip is celebrated on November 14, the focus of my attention was the *Menologia* for November or those that included that month.

In this connection it is important to note that a tenth-century author named Symeon revised and rewrote most of the Greek lives of the saints that were in use during his time, hence the moniker Symeon Metaphrastes—Symeon the "translator" or "rewriter."[3] Two factors provided the impetus for the revision of these texts: the evolution of the Greek language over the centuries and the development of Christian doctrine. Not every scribe, however, preferred Symeon's new versions to the older, premetaphrastic stories.[4] Out of the numerous *Menologia* for November, about 10 percent preserve older material on Philip, the so-called premetaphrastic version. The ecclesiastical requirement that the story of a saint's life be read on his or her feast day was often fulfilled in the case of an apostle by drawing from the last part of the ancient apocryphal Acts that recounted the saint's martyrdom. With regard to Philip, I found that among the fifty manuscripts with a premetaphrastic text, only five record a story different from what is called "The Act and Martyrdom of the Holy Apostle Philip." This other story, which recounts the apostle's activities in Athens, coincides with *Acts of Philip* 2 (BHG 1517).[5]

Sometimes when sorting through and studying these ancient documents even the difference of one letter in a title can have profound implications. For instance, the most common premetaphrastic title for the life of Philip is πρᾶξις καὶ μαρτύριον τοῦ ἁγίου ἀποστόλου Φιλίππου. But as I was working through the catalogue of Greek manuscripts at Mount Athos,[6] I found one place in the index where the plural πράξεις (Acts),

---

[3] See Christian Høgel, *Symeon Metaphrastes: Rewriting and Canonization* (Copenhagen: University of Copenhagen, Museum Tusculanum Press, 2002).

[4] The following two works are used extensively throughout this study: François Halkin, *Bibliotheca hagiographica graeca* (3d ed.; Subsidia hagiographica 8a; Brussels: Société des Bollandistes, 1957) = *BHG*; and François Halkin, *Novum Auctarium Bibliothecae hagiographicae graecae* (Subsidia hagiographica 65; Brussels: Société des Bollandistes, 1984). Each hagiographical text has a number; e.g., *BHG* 1527 is Symeon's document concerning the apostle Philip.

[5] See the critical edition by François Bovon, Bertrand Bouvier, and Frédéric Amsler, *Acta Philippi: Textus* (CCSA 11; Turnhout: Brepols, 1999). The five manuscripts are *Parisinus graecus 881* (P); *Vaticanus graecus 824* (V); *Vaticanus graecus 866* (X); the manuscript from Milan, *Ambrosianus graecus 450* (K); and the manuscript from Mount Athos, *Xenophontos 32* (A), which contains only the first lines of Act 2.

[6] Spyridōn Paulou Lambros, *Catalogue of the Greek Manuscripts on Mount Athos* (2 vols.; Cambridge: Cambridge University Press, 1895–1900; repr., Amsterdam: A. M. Hakkert, 1966).

instead of the singular πρᾶξις (Act), is used for a manuscript housed in the Monastery of Xenophontos. This was the initial moment of the exciting discovery of the least expurgated version of the *Acts of Philip* known to date, the one that we, Christopher Matthews and myself, are pleased to present here in English translation.

The manuscript, Athos, *Xenophontos 32* (A), consists of 141 folios of paper and dates to the fourteenth century C.E. The first and last two folios remain blank. The manuscript is incomplete, acephalous at the beginning and interrupted at the end. The content of folios 1r–29v is an *akolouthie* of St. Philip, that is, a series of prayers and other liturgical texts. These folios may once have had an independent existence, for at folio 30r there is a numbering of the quires, that is, a series of signatures, starting with the number 1 (α´). Folios 30r–123r originally consisted of sixteen quires, but some are now missing and some have been truncated. They contain the *Acts of Philip* (fols. 30r–92r), the *Martyrdom of Philip* according to recension Θ (fols. 92v–109v), and the *Praise of Philip* by Niketas the Paphlagonian (fols. 110r–123r); folio 124 remains blank. Next comes an acephalous version (missing the equivalent of one folio, recto and verso, at the beginning) of the text on St. Philip by Symeon Metaphrastes (fols. 125r–131r). The final text, written by another hand, is a liturgical fragment on St. Philip (fols. 132r–138bis), perhaps connected with the text of folios 1–29.

At folio 30r, the beginning of the *Acts of Philip*, there is a title specifying *Acts of Philip* 1 in epigraphical capital letters along with a decoration, a strip in the form of a portico. A marginal note at this point indicates that the book belongs to the monastery of Xenophontos. The following acts are marked with more modest strips or even the absence of any strip. At folio 92v, the *Martyrdom* account begins with a modest title, written in small capital letters along with accentuation, surmounted by a reticulated strip in the form of a portico. At folio 110r, the beginning of the *Praise of Philip* by Niketas, the title is still more modest in appearance—the letters are minuscules and the strip even smaller. These three texts—the *Acts*, the *Martyrdom*, and the *Praise*—constitute for the scribe an ensemble, indicated by the inclusion of an "amen" at the end of each text drawn in imitation of the way the Orthodox make the sign of the cross. At the end of the *Martyrdom* (fol. 109v) the scribe provides a colophon declaring that the text has been written "by the hand of the humble James, miserable and tattered." Unfortunately the identity of this scribe cannot be further established. After the *Akolouthie*, at the bottom of folio 29v, before the text of the *Acts* begins on the following folio, a scribe has inserted an instruction that the *Acts* should be read in the refectory while the *Martyrdom* should be read in the church.[7] The combination of scholarly trips to the "holy mountain," the *obligeance* of the authority of the Monastery of Xenophontos, particularly of their successive librarians, and the support of the Patristic Institute of the Monastery of Vlatadon in Thessaloniki in Greece prepared the way for a fruitful scholarly enterprise. In 1988 I published a long survey of the *Acts of Philip*.[8] A years-long collaboration from the seventies until today with Bertrand Bouvier, a scholar of classical and modern Greek language and literature, accompanied some years later by Frédéric Amsler, then a doctoral student and now a colleague in the study of early Christianity, made possible the publication of a critical edition of the *Acts of Philip* as well as its translation into French in 1999, in the Corpus Christianorum: Series Apocryphorum.[9] At the same time and as a companion volume to the edition of the Greek text, Amsler published his dissertation, which was a critical introduction to and commentary on the newly discovered *Acts of Philip*.[10]

While the European effort was under way, another research project was progressing in the United States. Under the aegis of Helmut

[7] For a more detailed description of the manuscript, see Bovon, Bouvier, and Amsler, *Acta Philippi: Textus*, xiii–xx.

[8] François Bovon, "Les Actes de Philippe," in *Aufstieg und Niedergang der römischen Welt* (II.25.6; ed. Wolfgang Haase and Hildegard Temporini; Berlin: de Gruyter, 1988), 4431–4527. Since then I have published the following studies: "Facing the Scriptures: Mimesis and Intertextuality in the *Acts of Philip*," in *Mimesis and Intertextuality in Antiquity and Christianity* (ed. Dennis R. MacDonald; SAC; Harrisburg, Pa.: Trinity Press International, 2001), 138–53; "Mary Magdalene in the *Acts of Philip*," in *Which Mary? The Marys of Early Christian Tradition* (ed. F. Stanley Jones; SBL Symposium Series 19; Atlanta: Society of Biblical Literature, 2002), 75–89; and "Women Priestesses in the Apocryphal *Acts of Philip*," in *Walk in the Ways of Wisdom: Essays in Honor of Elisabeth Schüssler Fiorenza* (ed. Shelly Matthews et al.; Harrisburg, Pa.: Trinity Press International, 2003), 109–21. These three last papers are reprinted in François Bovon, *New Testament and Christian Apocrypha* (WUNT 237; Tübingen: Mohr Siebeck, 2009), 246–85.

[9] See note 5. See also Frédéric Amsler, François Bovon, and Bertrand Bouvier, *Actes de l'apôtre Philippe* (Apocryphes 8; Turnhout: Brepols, 1996), with introduction and notes by Frédéric Amsler; Frédéric Amsler, François Bovon, and Bertrand Bouvier, "Actes de Philippe," in *Écrits apocryphes chrétiens* (vol. 1; Bibliothèque de la Pléiade 442; ed. François Bovon and Pierre Geoltrain; Paris: Gallimard, 1997), with introduction and notes by Frédéric Amsler, 1179–1320.

[10] Frédéric Amsler, *Acta Philippi: Commentarius* (CCSA 12; Turnhout: Brepols, 1999).

Koester, professor at Harvard Divinity School, and with the support of Demetrios Trakatellis, now Archbishop of the Greek Orthodox Church of America, Christopher Matthews was working on the Philip traditions that come to us from the first Christian centuries. He devoted an important chapter of his dissertation to the *Acts of Philip*, adding also in précis form an indication of the content of the ancient writing.[11] Matthews sought to show that the *Acts of Philip* in part grew out of earlier traditional stories and information associated with the name of the apostle Philip in the second century. Thus important continuities with such earlier traditions are present in the *Acts of Philip* together with new materials, the combination of which seems to have generated new stories that elaborated how Philip served to legitimate religious practices and convictions of the fourth century.

SCHOLARSHIP FROM THE SEVENTEENTH TO THE NINETEENTH CENTURY

The research that took place in the twentieth century would not have been possible without the work of previous generations of scholars, particularly the historians and philologists of the nineteenth century. As in many instances scholars rely on the pioneer work of the Bollandists, scholars of the Society of Jesus (Jesuits) devoted to hagiographic studies, who keep current a catalogue of all known Greek hagiographical documents. As early as 1680 the Bollandist Gottfried Henschen wrote a long notice on the apostle Philip in the *Acta Sanctorum*. He describes what was known about the apostle Philip's life and cult from Latin, Greek, and Oriental sources; focuses on Philip's daughters according to church authors; and includes an examination of Philip's relics. Then he presents four documents, the second one prepared by Daniel von Papenbrœck, another Bollandist: (1) a Latin life of Philip; (2) the Latin translation of Symeon Metaphrastes' piece on Philip; (3) the *Miracula s. Philippi*, a Latin translation of a passage from the great Greek Menaea for November 14 about Ireos (here called Heros), his wife, the Jew Aristarchos, and the young Theophilos whom the apostle raises from the dead; and (4) a story about the translation in 1204 of an arm of Philip from Jerusalem to Florence. Near the end of the same volume he provides the Greek text of a ὑπόμνημα of Saint Philip edited from a Vatican manuscript. This

---

[11] See Christopher R. Matthews, *Philip: Apostle and Evangelist. Configurations of a Tradition* (NovTSup 105; Leiden: Brill, 2002), 156–215.

is the text of Symeon Metaphrastes (*BHG* 1527), which had previously been translated into Latin.[12]

In 1851 Constantin Tischendorf first edited the *Martyrdom of Philip* (recension Γ) from *Parisinus graecus 881* (tenth century) and the Venetian *Marcianus graecus 349* (twelfth century), along with the story of Philip in Athens (*APh* 2) from *Parisinus graecus 881*.[13] Fifteen years later Tischendorf edited another form of the *Martyrdom*, recension Θ, according to codex *Parisinus graecus 1468* (eleventh century).[14] The Venetian manuscript already recorded the following title: "From the Peregrinations of Philip the apostle from the fifteenth of the Acts, in which is found the Martyrdom, until the end." This indicated that the *Martyrdom* had been extracted from a larger text. Moreover, scholars realized that the *Martyrdom* circulated in at least three forms, which are designated recensions Γ, Θ, and Δ. Several factors account for the differences among these recensions. Some of the discrepancies result from the fact that the *Martyrdom* was extracted from the end of the larger document at different starting points. In addition, a certain amount of rewriting was commonly involved with such a procedure.[15]

At the end of the nineteenth century, Maximilien Bonnet, the Swiss expert on the Apocrypha, discovered a larger portion of the *Acts of Philip* in *Vaticanus graecus 824* (V). In addition to the previously known *Martyrdom* and account of Philip in Athens (Act 2), it also included Acts 1 and 3 through 9. Although Pierre Batiffol quickly published an edition of the Greek text of the new Acts along with a Latin translation,[16]

---

[12] Gottfried Henschen and Daniel von Papenbrœck, eds., "De S. Philippo Apostolo Martyre Hieropoli Phrygia," in *Acta Sanctorum Maii* (vol. 1; Antwerp: Michaelis Cnobarum, 1680), 7–18 and 733–35. The introduction as well as the Metaphrastes Greek text along with the Latin translation are reproduced in the Migne collection (PG 115:183–98). Philip is presented on May 1, since the Bollandists present the saints according to the calendar of the Roman Catholic Church. The Catholic calendar changed in 1955 and again in 1969, and the apostle is celebrated today in the West on May 11.

[13] Constantin Tischendorf, *Acta apostolorum apocrypha* . . . (Leipzig: Avenarius et Mendelssohn, 1851), 75–104.

[14] Constantin Tischendorf, *Apocalypses apocryphae* . . . (Leipzig, 1866; repr., Hildesheim: Olms, 1966), 141–56.

[15] There is an English translation of the Martyrdom story according to recension Γ. See Alexander Walker's English translation: "Of the Journeyings of Philip the Apostle. From the Fifteenth Act until the End, and among Them the Martyrdom," in *The Ante-Nicene Fathers: The Writings of the Fathers Down to A.D. 325* (ed. Alexander Roberts and James Donaldson; vol. 8, 1895; repr., Peabody, Mass.: Hendrickson, 1994), 497–503.

[16] Pierre Batiffol, "Actus sancti Philippi Apostoli nunc primum edidit R. D. Petrus Batiffol," *Analecta Bollandiana* 9 (1890): 204–49.

Introduction   7

the subsequent text produced by Bonnet has remained the standard edition of the *Acts of Philip* for a century.[17] Bonnet's work was published in 1903 and is composed of the critical edition of the *Acts of Philip* based on *Vaticanus graecus 824*, the three forms of the *Martyrdom* (in a somewhat cumbersome presentation), and the first publication of a long part of the shorter form of the work as it is transmitted in *Parisinus graecus 1551* (fourteenth century).

Also at the end of the nineteenth century, Montague Rhodes James, the British specialist on early Christian Apocrypha, edited an account of the translation of Philip's relics from Ophiorymos to Hierapolis.[18] The manuscript that preserves this story, *Baroccianus graecus 180* (twelfth century) housed at Oxford in the Bodleian Library, presents the *Martyrdom* and the *Translation of the Relics* as one story without any sign of interruption.[19] It is not impossible that this document represents the primitive ending of the *Martyrdom*. Finally, in the first half of the twentieth century Albert Ehrhard examined and described many Greek manuscripts, and his unfinished work is still a gold mine of information. He was even aware of the *Xenophontos 32* manuscript, but his observation, confined to a footnote, remained unexploited.[20]

During the 1980s while I was working in the Bollandists' library in Brussels,[21] Michel van Esbroeck and François Halkin drew my attention to *Atheniensis 346* (G), a late fifteenth-century Greek manuscript from Athens that contains an independent document about Philip. Since it coincides partly with Act 8 of the *Vaticanus graecus 824* manuscript, we consider this piece to be a form of *Acts of Philip* 8. Moreover, each manuscript contains a long section that the other lacks.[22] Contrary to the rule of thumb followed by most New Testament scholars, the shorter form of a recension is not necessarily the most ancient. It seems that apocryphal texts were sometimes perceived by their readers to be overly redundant

---

[17] Maximilien Bonnet, "Acta Philippi et Acta Thomae, accedunt Acta Barnabae," in *Acta Apostolorum Apocrypha* (vol. 2.2; ed. Richard Adelbert Lipsius and Maximilien Bonnet; Leipzig: Mendelssohn, 1903; repr., Darmstadt: Wissenschaftliche Buchgesellschaft, 1959), 1–90.

[18] Montague Rhodes James, "Supplement to the Acts of Philip," in *Apocrypha Anecdota* (TS 2.3; ed. Montague Rhodes James; Cambridge: Cambridge University Press, 1893; repr., Nendeln, Liechtenstein: Kraus, 1967), 158–63.

[19] See Bovon, "Les Actes de Philippe," 4450–52.

[20] Ehrhard, *Überlieferung und Bestand*, 3:971.

[21] See note 4 above.

[22] See Bovon, Bouvier, and Amsler, *Acta Philippi: Textus*, 237–75.

8   The *Acts of Philip*

or even heretical in places. Consequently these texts were often abbreviated, either by a radical rewriting, as in the case of *Vaticanus graecus 824* in comparison with the much longer *Xenophontos 32*, or by an excision from their original contexts, as in the case of the three forms of the *Martyrdom* extracted from the larger complete *Acts*.

Over the long course of the editing and publishing of the *Acts of Philip* and related materials, little was done with regard to investigating the content or the origin of the *Acts of Philip*. The notable exceptions were the studies of Richard Adelbert Lipsius,[23] Joseph Flamion's analysis of the three forms of the *Martyrdom*,[24] and Erik Peterson's hypothesis concerning the social setting of the text. Peterson in particular insisted that there was a specific type of asceticism discernible in certain parts of the text. He found traces of the same spiritual attitude in encratite movements of the fourth and fifth centuries, visible in the literature of Messalianism and in the *Homilies* of Pseudo-Makarios.[25] The Cappadocian Fathers, particularly Basil of Caesarea, opposed that movement, judging it to promote an excessive form of asceticism.[26] In agreement with A. Lambert's and Georges Blond's research on fourth-century ascetical sects in Asia Minor such as the apotactic and the apostolic movements,[27] Peterson placed the *Acts of Philip* in the milieu of this ascetical literature of Asia Minor. This is still Amsler's conclusion and is shared in part by Matthews, with the proviso that some of the materials may predate this fourth-century redaction. This has also remained my opinion, with the same proviso, since the publication of my *Forschungsbericht* in 1988.[28]

[23] Richard Adelbert Lipsius, *Die apokryphen Apostelgeschichten und Apostellegenden. Ein Beitrag zur altchristlichen Literaturgeschichte* (2 vols. in 3 and supplement; Braunschweig: Schwetschke, 1884; repr., Amsterdam: Philo, 1976), 2.2:1–53, and *Ergänzungsband*, 64–73.

[24] Joseph Flamion, "Les trois recensions grecques du Martyre de l'apôtre Philippe," in *Mélanges d'histoire offerts à Charles Moeller: à l'occasion de son jubilé de 50 années de professorat à l'Université de Louvain. 1863–1913*. Vol. 1, *Antiquité et Moyen âge* (Université de Louvain. Recueil de travaux publiés par les membres des conférences d'histoire et de philologie 40; Louvain: Bureau du Recueil, 1914), 215–25.

[25] Erik Peterson, "Zum Messalianismus der Philippus-Akten," *OrChr*, 3d series, 7 (1932): 172–79; Peterson, "Die Häretiker der Philippus-Akten," *ZNW* 31 (1932): 97–111.

[26] Amsler, *Acta Philippi: Commentarius*, 469–520.

[27] A. Lambert, "Apotactites et Apotaxamènes," *Dictionnaire d'archéologie chrétienne et de liturgie*, vol. 1.2 (Paris: Letouzey et Ané, 1904), cols. 2604–26; Georges Blond, "L''hérésie' encratite vers la fin du quatrième siècle," *RSR* 32 (1944): 157–210.

[28] Amsler, *Acta Philippi: Commentarius*, 437–39; Matthews, *Philip: Apostle and Evangelist*, 196–97; Bovon, "Les Actes de Philippe," 4521–23.

Introduction   9

Sometimes, however, I wonder whether the text might not be older and related to the Montanist movement.[29]

Simultaneous with the scholarly work on the *Acts of Philip*, the religious tradition centered on Philip remained alive. Greek monks as they had done for centuries were still reading the old manuscripts, Metaphrastic and premetaphrastic forms of the *Acts of Philip*, on the saint's feast day, November 14. As important as the *Menologia* were and still are, the *Synaxaria* were also of vital importance. A *Synaxarium* presents the life of a saint in shorter form than the *Menologia*. Each local church possesses a *Synaxarium* in a unique form. One can read the shorter life of Saint Philip in the most famous *Synaxarium*, that of the Church of Constantinople, in the critical edition published by Hippolyte Delehaye in 1902.[30]

In 1982 a thick black notebook dated 1879 fell into my hands at the Monastery of Megisti Lavra on Mount Athos. Written in calligraphy, this book is filled with accounts of the lives of the apostles, written in modern *katharevousa* Greek by a monk from Saint Sabba, who came to Mount Athos at the end of his life.[31] This notebook, prepared by the monk Joaphas (surely with the hope of publication), is especially symbolic of the double religious and scholarly quest, given that it was produced during the same years that Constantin Tischendorf was preparing his first edition of the *Acts of Philip*.

THE MEMORY OF THE APOSTLE PHILIP
IN LATE ANTIQUITY

The Synoptic Gospels identify one of Jesus' twelve disciples as Philip but provide no details beyond his name and presence.[32] The Gospel of John adds some information about his origin (Bethsaida) and his interaction

---

[29] See below pp. 10–11. Matthews (*Philip: Apostle and Evangelist*, 23–27) remarks rightly that Philip and his daughters have been appropriated by the Montanists already in the second century C.E.

[30] Hippolyte Delehaye, *Synaxarium Ecclesiae Constantinopolitanae* (Brussels: Société des Bollandistes, 1902), 221–24.

[31] Athos, *Lavra Z 59*; see Bovon, "Editing the Apocryphal Acts of the Apostles," 17; and François Bovon, *Studies in Early Christianity* (WUNT 161; Tübingen: Mohr Siebeck, 2003), 209.

[32] Mark 3:18; Matt 10:3; Luke 6:14. See Matthews, *Philip: Apostle and Evangelist*, 95–100.

with Jesus.[33] In the lists of the twelve apostles Philip is associated with Bartholomew, and this companionship is preserved in the *Acts of Philip* (from *APh* 8 through the *Martyrdom*).[34] The canonical book of Acts not only offers a list of the apostles, including Philip and Bartholomew (Acts 1:13), but mentions another Philip among the seven Hellenists who were chosen to serve the Greek-speaking Christian community in Jerusalem (Acts 6:5). But this second Philip does not merely "wait on tables," but rather engages in missionary activity among the Samaritans, converts the magician Simon, and indirectly sends the gospel to Africa via an Ethiopian traveler (Acts 8:4-40). Later in the book, Luke describes this Philip as established in Caesarea Maritima, along with his four daughters who possessed the gift of prophecy (Acts 21:8-9).[35]

Second-century C.E. Greek Christian documents do not confirm the distinction between the two Philips, but speak of only one Christian leader with this name.[36] Papias (early second century C.E.) reports that he learned from the daughters of Philip about the raising of a dead person in association with Philip the apostle.[37] Polycrates of Ephesus (end of the second century C.E.) validated the Asian tradition concerning the date of Easter on the basis of Philip's apostolic authority. In response to the Romans, who argued for their date with reference to the presence in their city of the tombs of Peter and Paul, Polycrates asserted that the Asian churches also enjoyed an apostolic presence, namely the tomb of John in Ephesus and that of Philip in Hierapolis. He noted that Philip was buried in Hierapolis and had two daughters who remained virgins, while a third one lived in the Holy Spirit and rests in Ephesus.[38] About the same time the Montanist Proclus confidently responded to Roman

---

[33] See John 1:43-46; 6:5-7; 12:20-22; 14:8-11. See Matthews, *Philip: Apostle and Evangelist*, 100-126.

[34] See note 32 above and Acts 1:13.

[35] Matthews proposes the hypothesis that historically there was only one Philip (supported by the patristic evidence), and that Luke created the distinction (Luke 6:14 and Acts 1:13 for the apostle; Acts 6:1–8:40 and Acts 21:8-9 for the evangelist) to preserve his depiction of the apostles remaining in Jerusalem; see Matthews, *Philip: Apostle and Evangelist*, 33-34, 64-70, 94, 127-28.

[36] This material had been gathered already by Louis-Sébastien Le Nain de Tillemont, *Mémoires pour servir à l'histoire ecclésiastique des six premiers siècles* . . . , vol. 1 (2d ed.; Paris: Robustel, 1701), 383-86. See now Matthews, *Philip: Apostle and Evangelist*, 15-34.

[37] See Eusebius of Caesarea, *Hist. eccl.* 3.39.9; and Papias, frg. 10, preserved by Philip of Side.

[38] See Eusebius, *Hist. eccl.* 3.31.3 and 5.24.2.

claims about possessing "the sacred relics of the apostles"[39] by referring to the graves of the apostle Philip and those of his four daughters at Hierapolis in Asia.[40] Others, such as the anonymous "antimontanist" author (second to third centuries) cited by Eusebius, refused to admit any claim the Montanists made based on Philip's daughters.[41]

Clement of Alexandria adds some additional information about Philip and his daughters. First, he does not say that Philip actually suffered martyrdom; second, he implies that the apostle was married, since he had daughters; and third, he affirms that the apostle gave his daughters in marriage.[42] Clement's claims are polemically based: against Heracleon's declaration that some apostles while faithful did not end their lives as martyrs, and against Tatian's encratite opposition to marriage. That Philip was used as an authority by the Montanists, the gnostics, and the encratites probably explains why he and his *Acts* were not well received by the mainstream church.[43] It was among some of these marginal communities that the tradition of Philip's martyrdom developed and stories emerged that he had a sister rather than a wife and several daughters. The *Acts of Philip* bears witness to this other tradition. The climax of the work is the apostle Philip's martyrdom, and from Act 8 through the end no mention of daughters is made; the feminine presence around Philip rather is his sister named Mariamne.

One last bit of evidence must be mentioned here. In one of the third- to fourth-century *Manichaean Psalms*, the *Psalms of Heracleides*, Philip is said to have demonstrated the virtue of patience among the cannibals: "An enduring one is Philip, he being in the land of the Anthropophagi."[44] Although it is difficult to connect this remark with the Greek *Acts of Philip*, it is consistent with the Latin legend concerning Philip and James.[45] This reference to the *Manichaean Psalms* may serve as a transition to the next section, on the witnesses to the *Acts of Philip*.

---

[39] Eusebius, *Hist. eccl.* 2.25.6.
[40] Eusebius, *Hist. eccl.* 3.31.4.
[41] Eusebius, *Hist. eccl.* 5.17.2–3.
[42] Clement of Alexandria, *Strom.* 3.6.52.5; see also 4.9.71.2–3; Eusebius, *Hist. eccl.* 3.30.1.
[43] See Amsler, *Acta Philippi: Commentarius*, 8–9; Matthews, *Philip: Apostle and Evangelist*, 23–34.
[44] C. R. C. Allberry, ed., *A Manichean Psalm-Book: Part II* (Manichean Manuscripts in the Chester Beatty Collection 2; Stuttgart: Kohlhammer, 1932), 192, lines 10–11.
[45] See Bovon, "Les Actes de Philippe," 4437.

12   The *Acts of Philip*

It is certain indeed that the Manichaeans read the apocryphal Acts of the apostles with respect. Most likely they even created a corpus out of them.[46] The *Manichaean Psalms* confirm this veneration. They mention not only the apostles but also some other characters found in the apocryphal Acts, such as Thecla (*Acts of Paul*) and Maximilla (*Acts of Andrew*). It is probable, however, that they did not know the *Acts of Philip* as we have it, since the sentence quoted above is not consistent with the context of our *Acts*.[47]

In summary, although Philip did not receive as much attention as Peter, Paul, John, and Thomas, he was nevertheless acknowledged as a member of the apostolic collegium and venerated as both an apostle and a missionary.

KNOWLEDGE OF THE *ACTS OF PHILIP* IN BYZANTIUM AND IN THE WEST

The *Acts of Philip* lived a discreet life during the Byzantine centuries, as did the apostle himself.[48] As a member of the group of the twelve apostles, Philip was respected and his missionary stories beloved.[49] But given his appropriation by the Manichaeans and other heretical groups, he and the stories concerning his life were considered suspect. Besides the testimony of the scribes who copied the work, there are only a few references to the *Acts of Philip*, and these are late. An *Encomium* in honor of Philip (*BHG* 1530b) mentions explicitly the "book" of the *Acts of Philip*.[50] A

---

[46] See Éric Junod and Jean-Daniel Kaestli, *L'histoire des Actes apocryphes des apôtres du IIIe au IXe siècle: le cas des* Actes de Jean (Cahiers de la Revue de théologie et de philosophie 7; Lausanne: Revue de théologie et de philosophie, 1992), 50–86; and Knut Schäferdiek, "Die Leukios Charinos zugeschriebene manichäische Sammlung apokrypher Apostelgeschichten," in *Neutestamentliche Apokryphen in deutscher Übersetzung*, ed. Wilhelm Schneemelcher (2 vols.; 5th ed.; Tübingen: Mohr Siebeck, 1989), 2:81–93.

[47] See Amsler, *Acta Philippi: Commentarius*, 7–9; Matthews, *Philip: Apostle and Evangelist*, 15–34; Bovon, "Les Actes de Philippe," 4456–60.

[48] See still Lipsius, *Die apokryphen Apostelgeschichten und Apostellegenden*, 2.2:1–53.

[49] Later in the Byzantine period the Orthodox Church redivided Saint Philip: the apostle's date remained November 14, but the evangelist's date was fixed as October 11. In its notice in honor of the apostle, the *Synaxarium* of the Church of Constantinople relies on the apocryphal Acts, while for the evangelist it offers in about fifteen lines an account drawn exclusively from the canonical book of Acts. See Delehaye, *Synaxarium Ecclesiae Constantinopolitanae*, 129, 221–24.

[50] See Albert Frey, "L'Éloge de Philippe, saint apôtre et évangéliste du Christ (BHG 1530b)," *Apocrypha* 3 (1992): 165–209, esp. 184–85, lines 77–78.

work attributed to Anastasios the Sinaite, actually a Pseudo-Anastasios, contains a quotation from the *Acts of Philip*.[51] And without declaring his literary dependence, Nicetas the Paphlagonian (ninth century) in his homily on Saint Philip (*BHG* 1530), which is part of a series of homilies on the apostles, shows clearly that he uses the *Acts of Philip*.[52] The same is true of Symeon Metaphrastes (*BHG* 1527). What the rewriter says about Philip in the tenth century C.E. shows that he relies on the old *Acts of Philip*.[53] The same must be said of the person who produced an extended summary of the *Acts of Philip* (*BHG* 1528).[54]

A location of particular interest is Cyprus, and more precisely the small town of Arsos, where the cult of Philip and Mariamne developed starting in the thirteenth century. The martyrdom of Philip is celebrated every November 14, and the translation of his relics on July 31; Mariamne's day is February 17.[55] An icon from the early thirteenth century is preserved there and has recently been restored. Philip's portrait is surrounded by eighteen vignettes that depict several episodes in the life and martyrdom of the apostle. This icon proves that the *Acts of Philip* in a form close to *Xenophontos 32* and to the extended summary in *BHG* 1528 was known to the painter or at least to his patrons.[56] Over the centuries Arsos became a place of worship and pilgrimage. To this day people still come to Arsos with the expectation that they will be miraculously cured from various diseases and infirmities, particularly from earache.

In his *Historia ecclesiastica*, Nicephoros Callistos Xanthopoulos (beginning of the fourteenth century) also displays knowledge of traditions related to Philip the apostle.[57] Compared with the more numerous early testimonies related to the *Acts of John*, *Acts of Andrew*, *Acts of Peter*, *Acts of Paul*, and *Acts of Thomas*, these few witnesses at least show

---

[51] Pseudo-Anastasios, *De tribus quadragesimus, Sermo* 4, PG 89, 1396–97; see Bovon, "Les Actes de Philippe," 4452–53.

[52] Nicetas the Paphlagonian, *Oratio* 9, *In laudem sancti Philippi*, PG 105, 163–96; see Bovon, "Les Actes de Philippe," 4456.

[53] See Symeon Metaphastes, *Commentarius in sanctum Philippum apostolum*, PG 115, 187–98; see Høgel, *Symeon Metaphrastes*, 186; Bovon, "Les Actes de Philippe," 4444–45.

[54] See Bovon, "Les Actes de Philippe," 4445.

[55] See Delehaye, *Synaxarium Ecclesiae Constantinopolitanae*, 469.

[56] See François Bovon, "From Vermont to Cyprus: A New Witness of the *Acts of Philip*," *Apocrypha* 20 (2009): 9–27.

[57] Nicephoros Callistos Xanthopoulos, *Historia ecclesiastica*, 2.39, PG 145, 860–61.

that the *Acts of Philip* did not circulate widely and therefore was not well known. They also probably indicate that the *Acts of Philip*, like the *Martyrdom of Matthew* or the *Acts of Timothy*, is not as ancient and thus belongs to a "second wave" of literary production.[58]

In the West the author of the *Decretum Gelasianum* condemns a book with the title *Actus Philippi*. But we do not know whether this work was a Latin translation of the Greek *Acts of Philip* or the well-known Latin story (*BHL* 6814–17), which is very different from the Greek *Acts*.[59]

GREEK TEXTS RELATED TO THE APOSTLE PHILIP AND ANCIENT VERSIONS OF THE *ACTS OF PHILIP*

The literary history and form of hagiographical texts vary greatly from those of the fixed canonical writings. They also differ from those of the condemned apocryphal books.[60] The principal characteristic of hagiographical texts is their fluidity. It is, therefore, not surprising that we have two different extended forms of the *Acts of Philip* preserved in *Xenophontos 32* and *Vaticanus graecus 824*. Whereas *Vaticanus* is characterized by disciplined handwriting, correct spelling, and an orthodox orientation, *Xenophontos* is characterized by a scribe who is not attentive to elegant handwriting, correct spelling, or pure doctrine, but who respects the original deviant doctrine of the document.

As noted previously, the *Martyrdom* story has been transmitted in at least three different forms.[61] Another sign of diversity appears in the manuscript *Atheniensis 346*, which contains among other hagiographic, homiletical, and liturgical documents a variant form of *Acts of Philip* 8 as an isolated story followed by the *Martyrdom* (recension Γ).[62] Further examples of the fluid state of preservation are present in

---

[58] On the second wave, see Pierluigi Piovanelli, "Le recyclage des textes apocryphes à l'heure de la petite mondialisation de l'Antiquité tardive (ca. 325–451). Quelques perspectives littéraires et historiques," in *Poussières de christianisme et de judaïsme antiques. Études réunies en l'honneur de Jean-Daniel Kaestli et Éric Junod* (ed. Albert Frey and Rémi Gounelle; Publications de l'Institut romand des sciences bibliques 5; Prahins, Switzerland: Zèbre, 2007), 277–95. For another perspective, see Matthews, *Philip: Apostle and Evangelist*, 156–97, esp. 157–62.

[59] See below, p. 15.

[60] On this third category, see François Bovon, "Beyond the Canonical and the Apocryphal Books, the Presence of a Third Category: The Books Useful for the Soul," *HTR* 105 (2012): 125–37; and Bovon, *New Testament and Christian Apocrypha*, 318–22.

[61] These versions have been carefully analyzed by Flamion, "Les trois recensions grecques," 215–25.

[62] See Bovon, Bouvier, and Amsler, *Acta Philippi: Textus*, xxvi–xxx.

the summaries of the whole work such as those attested in *Parisinus graecus 1551* and *Mosquensis 161* (Vladimir 379; BHG 1528). Moreover, in the Greek *Menaen* of November published in Venice, a document is attached (BHG 1528f) that ignores Acts 8–15 and even the *Martyrdom*, but presents Acts 1–7 in an orthodox way.[63] The different forms found in the several *Synaxaria*, which make only brief or short mention of Philip, also provide proof that the *Acts of Philip*, even if not famous, was not ignored by Byzantine church and society.[64]

The lack of stability in the form of the text is confirmed when we move from Greek to other ancient languages. Here it is not even appropriate to speak of "versions," since most of the stories devoted to Saint Philip in other tongues do not correspond to the plot of the Greek *Acts*. In the Latin story (BHL 6814–17) Philip's missionary activity leads him to the country of the Scythians. Before his death, which does not come by martyrdom, the apostle defeats the cult of the pagan god Mars, represented by a dragon (dragons and snakes are a common element in the Greek, Coptic, and Syriac texts). In this Latin version Philip travels not with Bartholomew and Mariamne, but rather James the brother of the Lord, also called James the Minor. The memory of Philip and James the Minor was celebrated in the West on May 1 and not, as in the Byzantine world, on November 14. As attested by the *Legenda aurea*, this story was well known in the Middle Ages of Western Christianity.[65] Even today worshipers and visitors in Rome at the Church of the Holy Apostles can admire a very large painting by Muratori (1704) placed over the altar, which depicts Philip and James fighting against paganism.

There is also a Syriac story that shares little with the Greek *Acts* except for Philip's confrontation with a Jewish leader (BHO 974). Only fragments of the Coptic stories related to the apostle Philip are preserved (BHO 975–76 and 979). Readers of these fragments notice the influence of the Greek narrative (e.g., in the episode at the gate of the city, *APh* 13), but the whole document has been rewritten and adapted for the Coptic audience. The pairing of Philip and Mariamne is transformed into Philip and Peter, accommodating the Coptic interest in Peter as a figure

---

[63] See Bovon, "Les Actes de Philippe," 4445–46.
[64] See Bovon, Bouvier, and Amsler, *Acta Philippi: Textus*, xxvi–xxvii; Bovon, "Les Actes de Philippe," 4448–50.
[65] See James of Voragine, *La Légende dorée* (ed. Alain Boureau et al.; Bibliothèque de la Pléiade 504; Paris: Gallimard, 2004), 351–53. In James of Voragine's story, Philip the apostle is distinguished from Philip the evangelist and he dies as a martyr.

of authority and the influence of *Acts of Philip* 3, where Peter and those with him confirm Philip's activity. From the Coptic language the story was translated and adapted into Arabic and Ethiopic. The Armenian (*BHO* 980–81) and the Georgian texts are for their part regular translations of one form or another of the *Martyrdom*, the last part of the *Acts of Philip*. The memory of Philip is also preserved in Irish and Old Slavonic.[66]

THE STRUCTURE AND ORIGIN OF THE *ACTS OF PHILIP*

If one can trust the witness of the manuscripts, the *Acts of Philip* was known and distributed under two different titles: *Acts of the Holy Apostle Philip* and *Journeys of the Holy Apostle Philip*.[67] This variation in the title perhaps already reflects the composite nature of the work. The evidence for this is best described from a broad chronological perspective. During the initial period the *Acts* grew on the basis of the merging of several earlier documents. Then in the second phase the *Acts* diminished. We have noted already the evidence for the extraction of the *Martyrdom* from the rest of the work to serve as a reading for the feast day of the apostle. If *Acts of Philip* 2 did not have an independent existence, it may have been extracted in a similar way.

The expansion of the work in the first period of production must now be explained. As it stands in *Vaticanus graecus 824* and even more clearly in *Xenophontos 32*, the content of the *Acts of Philip*—the title standing at the head of the text[68]—gives the strong impression of being an amalgamation of different sources. Matthews, Amsler, and myself are in agreement here. Only the sequence from *Acts of Philip* 8 through the *Martyrdom* constitutes a unity. Here we find the episodic story of an apostolic group composed of Philip, Bartholomew, and Mariamne, accompanied for some time by a pair of talking animals, a kid goat and a leopard, on a single missionary journey to the city of Ophioryme (or Ophiorymos). According to the majority of the manuscripts, Ophioryme is another name for the major Phrygian city Hierapolis (modern Pammukale).

---

[66] On all these versions, see Bovon, "Les Actes de Philippe," 4437–43.

[67] Bovon, "Les Actes de Philippe," 4466–67. The list in the Pseudo-Gelasius *Decretum* mentions the work as *Actus nomine Philippi apostoli apocryphi*; see Ernst von Dobschütz, *Das Dekretum Gelasianum de libris recipiendis et non recipiendis in kritischem Text herausgegeben und untersucht* (TU 38.4; Leipzig: J. C. Hinrichs, 1912), 11, 50, 72, 83, and 291 n. 1.

[68] The title in fol. 30r of the manuscript *Xenophontos 32*.

Introduction 17

Bartholomew and Mariamne, as well as the animals, are absent from *Acts of Philip* 1-7. The episodes in this first part, with the exception of Acts 5-7, are loosely integrated and lack the unity that characterizes Act 8 through the *Martyrdom*. *Acts of Philip* 1 is in part a resurrection account reminiscent of stories of Elijah (1 Kgs 17:17-24) and Elisha (2 Kgs 4:8-37) and influenced by the story of Jesus raising the only son of the widow from Nain (Luke 7:11-17). It perhaps fits with Papias' allusion to a miraculous resurrection connected with Philip and his daughters (the passage preserved by Eusebius of Caesarea, *Hist. eccl.* 3.39.9, is not quite clear).[69] Within the frame of this resurrection account is an extended "tour of hell" related by the boy Philip calls back to life.

Acts of Philip 2, Philip's dispute with the philosophers in Athens, constitutes an independent literary unit. It lacks any sign of excessive asceticism and lacks heretical elements. It seems to be an orthodox construction with material incorporating other parts of the *Acts*, such as Philip's controversy with a Jew (see *APh* 6.9-15) inserted into the dispute with the philosophers, and the punishment of the opponents including their being swallowed up by the earth (see *Acts of Philip Martyrdom* 26-28).[70]

Acts of Philip 3 seems to be the beginning of a story relative to the evangelist Philip. Reading perhaps too much into the text, I see it as the equivalent of canonical Acts 8, but instead of the new convert Simon needing Peter's additional spiritual gift, here it is Philip who needs the supplement of grace to become fully equipped as an apostle. From this perspective it might be suggested that *Acts of Philip* 1-7 concerns Philip the evangelist and stands in conversation with the canonical Book of Acts.[71] The connection with Acts 8 is also attested by several topographic

---

[69] See Enrico Norelli, ed., *Papia di Hierapolis: Esposizione degli oracoli del signore. I frammenti. Introduzione, testo, traduzione e note* (Letture cristiane del primo millennio 36; Milan: Paoline, 2005), 230-335, esp. 284-89.

[70] Matthews has a different opinion. In his view the debate with the high priest is the major narrative thread, and the philosophers enter the scene to intertextually recall Acts 17; in this case *Acts of Philip* 2 would be a rewriting using the other elements and not so much an insertion. See Matthews, *Philip: Apostle and Evangelist*, 186-89; and Amsler, *Acta Philippi: Commentarius*, 94-103.

[71] Matthews (*Philip: Apostle and Evangelist*, 166-71) disputes this view, arguing that there is little evidence apart from Act 3 and the thematic connection at the beginning of Act 4 to support the view that anyone other than Philip the apostle is intended in the rest of Acts 1-7. Given that later ecclesiastical tradition distinguishes between the two Philips more clearly than do second-century sources, one would expect an explicit naming of

and geographic details found in *Acts of Philip* 3 and the beginning of *Acts of Philip* 4. Thus the city of Azotus appears here (*APh* 4.1), just as it is present in the canonical Acts in relation to Philip the evangelist (Acts 8:40). And just as the same Philip converts and baptizes the Ethiopian eunuch, high civil servant of the Candace, the queen of Ethiopia (Acts 8:26-40), in the *Acts of Philip* the hero is supposed to have traveled by sea as far as the border of the Candacean people (*APh* 3.10).

Similar in some respects to *Acts of Philip* 1, *Acts of Philip* 4 constitutes a single independent story, recounting the healing of a young woman and her conversion, as well as the baptism of her parents.

Acts of Philip 5-7 belong together as parts of a continuing story. Philip's convert, the wise Ireos, accepts the message of the gospel as well as the messenger. As often happens in apocryphal Acts of the apostles, such a conversion does not take place without some family turmoil. This is the case here, as Ireos' wife does not immediately accept her husband's new way of life and the hospitality he offers to the apostle. Then, when Philip is threatened by the city authorities and attacked by Aristarchos, a leading Jew, Ireos takes on the role played by Gamaliel in the canonical Acts of the Apostles (Acts 5:33-42) and protects the apostle. Philip emerges as victorious over Aristarchos because he is able to raise the young Theophilos from the dead. The last part of the cycle, *Acts of Philip* 7, features the construction of a church, termed an "assembly hall" (συναγωγή) in 7.2 and 7.4, to host the new Christian community. This may have been a subsequent addition to the literary unit devoted to Ireos.[72] Comparison of the two manuscripts, *Xenophontos 32* and *Vaticanus graecus 824*, is always instructive. It is not surprising that the Vatican codex as an orthodox revision of an earlier heretical story omits the encratite meal and mentions a normal catechetical teaching, followed by baptism in the name of the Holy Trinity sharing the same essence (ὁμοούσιος is used). The Athos codex simply states, "Then the disciples prepared bread and vegetables, because Philip had said, 'After my victory I will break my fast, rejoicing exceedingly in my Christ'" (*APh* 6.22).

Acts of Philip 8, as already noted, constitutes a new beginning and recounts the calling and commissioning of Philip. The author respects

---

Philip the evangelist in the *Acts of Philip* were that figure intended at any point. Rather, data from Acts 8 have been employed to fill out the profile of the apostle.

[72] See Amsler, *Acta Philippi: Commentarius*, 271-84.

Introduction   19

an old tradition according to which the apostles were afraid to begin their missionary task and needed some "encouragement."[73] This caring exhortation is foreseen by the Lord and entrusted to Mariamne, just as it is given by the savior to Mary Magdalene in other noncanonical writings.[74] Mariamne indeed plays the role of Mary Magdalene as her name already suggests, since Μαριάμνη is one of the three possible Greek forms for the Hebrew *Myriam*, that is, Mary.[75] *Acts of Philip* 8 is truncated after only a few lines in codex *Xenophontos 32*, but is partially preserved in *Vaticanus graecus 824* (§§1-6 and 15-21), as well as in *Atheniensis 346* (§§1-15), which gives the title as "Act of the holy apostle Philip in which the lots of the holy apostles are assigned," without indicating a number. After a beginning that is shared by the two codices (§§1-6), the Athenian manuscript preserves the totality of a dialogue between the risen Christ and the apostle Philip (§§3-14), while the Vatican manuscript, after a paragraph common to both manuscripts (§5), preserves the meeting of the apostles with the two animals at the end of the Act (§§16-21).

The conversion of the animals and their travels together with the apostolic band fill the following Acts (*Acts of Philip 9-Martyrdom*). The partial transformation of animals into standing and speaking creatures is a well-known folkloristic motif.[76] The biblical female donkey rebuking Balaam (Num 22:21-35) and the wild mules in the *Acts of Thomas* 70-81 are earlier examples.[77] A later parallel to our story is found in an Athonite legend about a young shepherd, John Koukouzelis, who went on to become a famous Byzantine church musician. It is said that he played the flute so well that the lambs and goats of his flock stood on their hind legs.[78] The notion of the conversion of animals should not be

---

[73] See the Manichean Psalm of Heracleides in Allberry, *Manichean Psalm-Book*, 187.

[74] See the *Gospel of Mary* 15.1-15; or 9.2-26 according to Karen L. King, *The Gospel of Mary: Jesus and the First Woman Apostle* (Santa Rosa, Calif.: Polebridge, 2003).

[75] See François Bovon, "Mary Magdalene's Paschal Privilege," in Bovon, *New Testament Traditions and Apocryphal Narratives*, trans. Jane Haapiseva-Hunter (Allison Park, Pa.: Pickwick, 1995), 147-57, 228-35; Bovon, "Mary Magdalene in the *Acts of Philip*," 75-89.

[76] See Christopher R. Matthews, "Articulate Animals: A Multivalent Motif in the Apocryphal Acts of the Apostles," in Bovon, Brock, and Matthews, *Apocryphal Acts of the Apostles*, 205-32.

[77] See also *Acts of Thomas* 39-41, the speaking kid donkey.

[78] I received this information from Bertrand Bouvier during a stay at Mount Athos.

reduced simply to the naïveté of popular religion, insofar as this motif addresses the issue of the extent of Christian redemption, as indeed one of the speaking animals in the text asserts. The author of these legends insists that the animal world is not excluded from Christ's salvation, that redemption is not limited to the human realm.[79]

The textual tradition suggests that such ideas were too much for some readers of the *Acts of Philip*. At some point one of the users of the *Xenophontos 32* manuscript was apparently so offended by some passages of *Acts of Philip* 9–11 that he gave full force to his execration by tearing away a section of the book. The result of this violent reaction is that twenty-four folios are now missing, and a search for them in the library of the Xenophontos monastery was unfortunately in vain.[80] For *Acts of Philip* 9 we are entirely dependent on the revised, short form of *Vaticanus graecus 824*. The whole of *Acts of Philip* 10 is lost, as is also the first part of *Acts of Philip* 11. It is probable that in the lacuna the baptism of the animals was recounted,[81] which can be inferred from *Acts of Philip* 12 where the animals are not fully satisfied and express their wish to take part in the Eucharist.

After the lacuna, when the text of *Xenophontos 32* begins again in *Acts of Philip* 11, it presents an account of a victory over a monster and fifty demons, followed by a liturgy of communion. This is the eucharistic service that initiates the complaint by the two animals who are eager to participate as well. But this liturgical portion of the text is significant for another reason. To the surprise of the reader the prayer that is spoken is a rewritten version of the Hymn of Christ in the *Acts of John*.[82] This part of the *Acts of John* is found in only one Greek manuscript preserved in the National Library at Vienna (*hist. gr.* 63). The hymn was known,

---

[79] See François Bovon, "The Child and the Beast: Fighting Violence in Ancient Christianity," *HTR* 92 (1999): 369–92, esp. 373; see also Matthews, "Articulate Animals."

[80] See Bovon, Bouvier, and Amsler, *Acta Philippi: Textus*, xiv.

[81] See Amsler, *Acta Philippi: Commentarius*, 340–43. As a parallel we have the story of the baptism of a lion in the recently published Coptic fragment of Bodmer Papyrus X. See Rodolphe Kasser and Philippe Luisier, "Le Papyrus Bodmer XLI en édition princeps. L'épisode d'Éphèse des *Acta Pauli* en copte et en traduction," *Le Muséon* 117 (2004): 281–384. The end of the story was known already through the Hamburg Greek papyrus; see Willy Rordorf et al., "Actes de Paul," in Bovon and Geoltrain, *Écrits apocryphes chrétiens*, 1:1123 and 1:1156. See also Matthews, "Articulate Animals," 206–10.

[82] *Acts of John*, 94–96. On this hymn, see Éric Junod and Jean-Daniel Kaestli, *Acta Iohannis* (vol. 2; CCSA 2; Turnhout: Brepols, 1983), 632–55; on its reinterpretation in the *Acts of Philip*, see Amsler, *Acta Philippi: Commentarius*, 348–54.

however, by Augustine. The Priscillianists in Spain and Portugal during the fourth and fifth centuries appreciated and read apocryphal texts. In fact, Priscillian himself wrote an apology defending apocryphal literature. They also knew and recited in particular this Hymn of Christ. Confronted with this circumstance, a bishop by the name of Ceretius sent two suspect books to Augustine and requested his assessment. In his response the African theologian, who may have become acquainted with the hymn during his nine years as a member of the Manichaean movement, refused to confer any authority upon it.[83] The witness to the hymn afforded by the *Acts of Philip* is important since there are otherwise very few references to it from antiquity. It must be noted that the author of the *Acts of Philip* has transformed the role of Christ, who in the *Acts of Philip* is the object of the prayer.

The process employed in the *Acts of Philip* to rewrite an ancient document—here the Hymn of Christ—is probably not unusual. Even if their sources cannot be identified, the many prayers that appear in the *Acts of Philip* were probably not composed by the author or—more correctly—the authors themselves. As frequently happened with liturgical documents, the authors probably recycled ancient prayers. Indeed, a careful reading of both the prayers and the narrative parts of the *Acts of Philip* reveals a difference in the style of their language. The prayers are recorded in a more sophisticated style than the very simple and popular mode of the narrative sections. There is a good chance that they are incorporated as quotations, though evidently not without some adjustments.[84] This circumstance bestows special value on the *Acts of Philip*. For even if the final form of the *Acts* is late (fourth century C.E.), some portions of the content derive from earlier times and bring to light archaic (second to third century C.E.) Christian liturgical material.

In the present form of *Xenophontos 32*,[85] the Eucharist is offered only to Bartholomew and Mariamne (*APh* 11.10; see 11.1), while the animals are granted an aspersion of holy water (*APh* 12). It may be, however, that the earlier form had granted full communion to the leopard

---

[83] See Augustine, *Epist. 237 ad Ceretium*, CSEL 57, 526–32; Junod and Kaestli, *L'histoire des Actes apocryphes des apôtres*, 90–94; also Junod and Kaestli, *Acta Iohannis*, 2:646–47.

[84] For examples of such prayers, see *Acts of Philip* 2.13; 3.4; 3.13; 4.2; 8.19; 9.4; 11.9; 12.7; 13.5; 14.5; 15.7; *Martyrdom* 26; 38.

[85] *Vaticanus graecus 824* does not have this part of the story, but skips from Act 9 to the *Martyrdom*.

and the kid goat.[86] From Amphilochius of Iconium, who wrote against the heretics and their use of apocryphal texts, we have an enigmatic affirmation that some members of a sect had animals.[87] This affirmation may be read as an allusion to the incorporation of animals into the Christian community. Indeed, throughout the history of Christianity there have been efforts to bless the animal world and to affirm that the rays of the Christian hope of salvation shine upon it.[88]

Acts of Philip 9 and 11 tell of two apostolic encounters with dragons that bear certain similarities to one another, though we probably have to do with distinct creatures in each case.[89] Again such formidable fights belong to the arena of popular legend and folklore. One should not for this reason, however, neglect the religious perspective of such victories. The book of Revelation pits the positive triad of God, the Lamb, and the Seven Spirits (see Rev 1:4-5) against the negative triad of Satan/the Dragon, the Beast from the Sea, and the Beast from the Earth.[90] Such confrontations have cosmic and apocalyptic dimensions, evident in the case of the *Acts of Philip* through the physical descriptions of the monsters and the naming of their ancestors. With respect to the latter instance, the dragon of *Acts of Philip* 11 traces its origin back to paradise and the fall in a manner reminiscent of the dragon in the *Acts of Thomas* that explains its origin and that of evil itself.[91]

Preserved only in *Xenophontos 32*, *Acts of Philip* 13 presents another successful fight of the apostle. In this scene one discovers that the city of Ophioryme, the destination of the apostolic band, is protected by some mysterious security measures. Each of the seven guards at the border carries a snake on his shoulders that will strike unwanted visitors. The criterion for safe passage is whether or not one is recognized

---

[86] See Matthews, "Articulate Animals," 225-31.

[87] See Frédéric Amsler, "Amphiloque d'Iconium, Contre les hérétiques encratites et apotactites. Traduction française," in Frey and Gounelle, *Poussières de christianisme et de judaïsme antiques*, 7-40, esp. 23.

[88] See Andrew Linzey, *Animal Theology* (Urbana: University of Illinois Press, 1995); Paul Waldau and Kimberley Patton, eds., *A Companion of Subjects: Animals in Religion, Science, and Ethics* (New York: Columbia University Press, 2006). On the motif in apocryphal literature that Christian salvation includes animals as well as human beings, see Matthews, "Articulate Animals."

[89] See Bovon, "Child and the Beast."

[90] See Revelation 12-13; François Bovon, "Les institutions romaines selon l'Apocalypse de Jean," *CNS* 7 (1986): 221-38, esp. 224-29.

[91] *Acts of Thomas* 31-33; see Amsler, *Acta Philippi: Commentarius*, 326-48.

as participating in the cult of the Viper. Philip, Bartholomew, and Mariamne, however, are protected by divine power, and the snakes are unable to strike at them. This success is followed by the destruction of two great dragons who guard the city gates through the most potent weapon of the apostolic team, the ray of light of the Monad (*APh* 13.3).

Frédéric Amsler has developed an innovative socioreligious explanation for the portrayal of the victory over the Viper and her devotees.[92] Interested in transitions from one religion to another, he examined instances in which layers of successive cults can be detected at the same sacred site (e.g., the young Apollo who is victorious over the old snake Pytho at Delphi). Strabo's descriptions as well as archaeological evidence indicate that such a transition took place at Hierapolis of Phrygia.[93] The old Anatolian cult of Cybele gave way to the new Greek cult of Apollo, and a Greek temple was built over the Anatolian cave. The *Acts of Philip* continues the defeat of Cybele, but this time to the benefit of the Christian God. Philip's opponent, however, is not Apollo but Cybele. Amsler contends that the Viper is a symbolic reference to Cybele and that the leopard and the kid goat also belong in the company of the goddess. This latter point seems to go too far, for the choice of these two animals is determined above all by the description of paradise and eschatological peace in the book of Isaiah (Isa 11:6-9 and 65:25). Amsler accepts the connection to Isaiah but enlarges the cultural relationships in the *Acts of Philip* to include Anatolian cults as well.

At this point the narrative continuity of the *Acts of Philip* becomes somewhat disrupted, for although the victory over the cult of the Viper, the principal cult of the city, is mentioned here and there in the text, it is never described in a broader context.[94] It may have been the core of the original story, now lost. In the Greek forms of the *Acts of Philip*, what provokes Philip's martyrdom is not an attack upon the local center of worship but the preaching of sexual abstinence, which is accepted by Nicanora, the governor's wife. But before reaching that point in *Acts of*

---

[92] See Frédéric Amsler, "The Apostle Philip, the Viper, the Leopard, and the Kid: The Masked Actors of a Religious Conflict in Hierapolis of Phrygia (*Acts of Philip* VII–XV and *Martyrdom*)," in *Society of Biblical Literature 1996 Seminar Papers* (SBL Seminar Papers 35; Atlanta: Society of Biblical Literature, 1996), 432–37; Amsler, *Acta Philippi: Commentarius*, 299–312 and 521–42.

[93] Strabo, *Geography* 13.4.14.

[94] It is very present in the Latin legend of Philip and James.

Philip 15, *Acts of Philip* 14 relates the miraculous story of Stachys, the old blind man, who is healed by the apostle.[95]

The name of Stachys is preserved in the Greek Orthodox liturgy since his story constitutes the beginning of the notice about the apostle Philip read from the *Synaxarium* on the apostle's feast day, November 14.[96] Stachys' story contains several notable elements.[97] From the point of view of the history of medicine, the efforts of Stachys' wife to gather the early morning dew to relieve her husband's pain are noteworthy (*APh* 14.3).[98] From the point of view of religious experience, Stachys' dreams and visions are imposing. In a prophetic vision the old man contemplates a divine apparition, embedded not in the Christian notion of the Trinity, but more probably in the Egyptian or Palmyrean image of the divine triad (father–mother–child)—he contemplates an old man, a woman, and a boy.

Acts of Philip 15 contains the tale of Nicanora, the governor's wife who is also cured by Philip. Her conversion to the apostle's faith provokes the jealousy and wrath of her husband, the cruel Tyrannognophos.

All three forms of the *Martyrdom*—the last part of the *Acts of Philip*—attest to the traditional triangulation, well known through the *Acts of Andrew*, the *Acts of Paul*, the *Acts of Peter*, and the *Acts of Thomas*:[99] the encratite missionary preaching of the apostle converts one or several women who then decline the sexual expectations of their husbands or lovers. This attitude enrages the husband or the lover, usually a high political figure, who precipitates and then brings to completion the persecution and the martyrdom of the apostle. Thus in the *Acts of Philip*

---

[95] As is the case with *Acts of Philip* 11–13, *Acts of Philip* 14–15 are preserved only by the manuscript *Xenophontos 32*. Amsler (*Acta Philippi: Commentarius*, 383–428) suggests that the excerpting of the *Martyrdom* to create an independent liturgical legend (see the many manuscripts that preserve only this part of the work) affected the plot of *Acts of Philip* 14 and 15 in *Xenophontos 32*. It is true that the present interweaving of the stories of Stachys and Nicanora in *Acts of Philip* 14 and 15 does not seem to have preserved the original narrative sequence. According to Amsler *Acts of Philip* 15.2-3 and probably *Acts of Philip* 15.4, if not *Acts of Philip* 15.5, originally belonged to *Acts of Philip* 14, insofar as they are devoted to Stachys and not to Nicanora.

[96] See Delehaye, *Synaxarium Ecclesiae Constantinopolitanae*, 221–24.

[97] *Acts of Philip* 14.1–9.

[98] Amsler's source-critical reconstruction of the origin of *Acts of Philip* 14 and 15 (*Acta Philippi: Commentarius*, 383–405) is not entirely convincing.

[99] Justin's *Second Apology* 2.1–20 proves that such a situation is plausible on the sociohistorical level. It tells of a case at Alexandria in which a husband puts on trial a certain Ptolomeus, the Christian instructor of his wife.

Nicanora's conversion ignites Tyrannognophos' fury and sets in motion the apostle's arrest, trial, and condemnation. One interesting aspect of the scenario in the *Acts of Philip* is the role played by Mariamne.[100] This female missionary is very active during the journey, and in Ophioryme she preaches, baptizes, and speaks to Nicanora. Both women converse in the same Semitic language, since Nicanora is also of Semitic origin (she arrived in Asia Minor after an accident at sea, having washed up on the shoreline). In their present form, the three versions of the *Martyrdom* story limit Mariamne's preaching activity. She calls the people from the street, but then leads them inside where they listen to a sermon delivered by Philip. In the earlier form of the text—the disruptions in the textual tradition speak in favor of an earlier lost form of the narrative—Mariamne probably, like Thecla, was portrayed as preaching to women as Philip was preaching to men. She was like the preaching Wisdom figure in Proverbs 8. In the present form of the text the picture of the baptismal activity of Mariamne leading the women into the water while Philip is baptizing the men seems to confirm this hypothesis.

It is worth underlining that several sects in fourth-century Phrygia, such as the apotactites and the apostolics, according to their patristic opponents as well as their own funeral inscriptions, maintained parallel ministerial offices for men and women, not only at the level of deacon and deaconess but also at the levels of priest and bishop. This illuminates a key apologetic and paraenetic function of the *Acts of Philip*. Male and female ministers of these marginal religious communities found an authoritative model for their identity in the historical memory of Philip and Mariamne's apostolic mission. It is not by chance that Mariamne is the "sister" of Philip, rather than his wife, his mother, or his daughter. Both she and he are related through a strong bond outside sexual attachment.[101] The presence in the text of Bartholomew, whose activity is rather modest, may be taken as the necessary token of respect paid to the New Testament lists of the twelve.

Besides the conventional elements of a martyrdom story, the narrative presents a special scene in which Philip loses his temper and curses his persecutors from the cross. In returning evil for evil, concretely by sending his opponents, the citizens of the town, the priests, and even the governor into the abyss, the apostle disobeys the commandment of

---

[100] See Bovon, "Mary Magdalene in the *Acts of Philip*"; Bovon, "Women Priestesses."
[101] See Bovon, "Women Priestesses," 118–21.

his Lord. An appearance of the risen Christ gives the author the opportunity to quote a long sequence of Jesus' sayings. In my opinion, this rhetorical sequence is not an invention of the author, but a quotation of a lost collection of Jesus' sayings whose genre is paralleled by the *Gospel of Thomas*.[102]

The Savior's decision to punish the irascible apostle and to announce the nature of the punishment is important in view of the history of Orthodox piety. Philip, the apostle and the martyr, will not have immediate access to paradise after his death but will have to remain penitent for a period of forty days. This augmentation of the plot probably has a liturgical origin. In the Greek Orthodox tradition, the second most important period of fasting after Lent is the forty days before the celebration of Jesus' birth. Even today this period begins on November 14, the feast day of Saint Philip, and is identified by the nomenclature "the fasting period of Saint Philip."[103] It is very likely that the *Martyrdom* of Saint Philip appends this additional episode to offer legitimization of this special period of fasting.

Another issue that must be discussed is whether Ophioryme and Hierapolis are two names for a single city or whether they designate two different sites. The tendency in the manuscript tradition is to consider the two names as designations for the same city. The story of the *Translation of the Relics*, on the contrary, distinguishes them clearly. Although scholars usually follow the opinion of the majority of manuscripts, in this case it seems preferable to suggest that in the beginning the martyrdom took place in Ophioryme, which seems to be an imaginary location, while the burial place was in the city of Hierapolis. Patristic evidence, as we have seen, names Hierapolis as the city where Philip's tomb is located.[104]

---

[102] On this genre, see James M. Robinson, "ΛΟΓΟΙ ΣΟΦΩΝ: On the Gattung of Q," in James M. Robinson and Helmut Koester, *Trajectories through Early Christianity* (Philadelphia: Fortress, 1971), 71–113. On this passage, see François Bovon, "The Synoptic Gospels and the Noncanonical Acts of the Apostles," *HTR* 81 (1988): 19–36, esp. 30–31.

[103] Karl Holl, "Die Entstehung der vier Fastenzeiten in der griechischen Kirche," in *Abhandlungen der Berliner Akademie der Wissenschaften 1923* (Philosophisch-historische Klasse 5); repr., Holl, *Gesammelte Aufsätze zur Kirchengeschichte*, vol. 2, *Der Osten* (Tübingen: Mohr Siebeck, 1928), 155–203.

[104] See above, pp. 10–11.

THE SPIRITUAL WORLD OF THE *ACTS OF PHILIP*

The text permits us to construct a portrait of the faith of the author or authors and more broadly his or their spirituality. Jesus Christ is a divine and active savior close to God. By his power he provides humanity with an opportunity for salvation in a transcendent world.[105] His apostles participate in his progressive triumph, and in a paradoxical way they succeed in performing tangible miracles, even resurrections of the dead. But these strong and material arguments serve a transcendent and spiritual goal: eternal life in another world.[106] This life is divided between the good and the bad. The presence of monsters proves that human sinfulness is only one aspect of the decrepitude of this world. The divine redeemer practices mercy but also practices retribution. Morality is required from all believers, and Philip's weakness in this regard is condemned.

In this conception of spirituality, special access to divine truth must be demonstrated. In addition to the positive response of faith believers make to the proclamation of the Christian gospel, they must also demonstrate spiritual movement toward religious perfection. Thus the religious community behind and in the *Acts of Philip* proposes a spiritual program beyond simple faith. Such a spiritual way is attested in the homilies of Pseudo-Makarios and the Messalian movement, and also finds expression here and there in the *Acts of Philip*. The term ἁγνεία ("purity" or "continence") plays an important role in this respect. Through such ethical efforts and spiritual exercises, through ἁγνεία as the text says, believers have access to God—they can even see God.[107] A vision of God, then, is by no means impossible. On the contrary, it may be achieved through a certain spiritual attitude. Mainstream Christianity, represented in fourth-century Asia Minor by Basil of Caesarea and Amphilochius of Iconium, opposed such a claim. Why? This is not quite clear. Were the church leaders afraid of too much asceticism? Were they convinced that such a vision of God could only be an illusion? Was their opposition the expression of social or political hostility?

---

[105] See François Bovon and Éric Junod, "Reading the Apocryphal Acts of Apostles," in *The Apocryphal Acts of Apostles* (ed. Dennis Ronald MacDonald; Semeia 38; Decatur, Ga.: Scholars Press, 1986), 161–71, esp. 167–69.

[106] David Pao, "Physical and Spiritual Restoration: The Role of Healing Miracles in the *Acts of Andrew*," in Bovon, Brock, and Matthews, *Apocryphal Acts of the Apostles*, 259–80.

[107] See *Acts of Philip* 1.3 and 4.1.

LANGUAGE

The narratives brought together in the *Acts of Philip* are written in a popular Koine Greek, which is correct but rudimentary in vocabulary, syntax, and style. While modern scholars might complain about these formal weaknesses, they may also rejoice over having such exceptional access to the written expression of simple Christian believers of late antiquity. Noncanonical literature is precious because it preserves a good portion of the popular writings that survive from antiquity.[108] The only passages of higher literary quality (rhythmic enumeration, original images, alliterations, original metaphors) found in the *Acts* are the prayers pronounced by the apostle before or after a miracle, an ordeal, or a decisive endeavor. As mentioned above, these prayers are very likely insertions of more ancient material, incorporated with some adjustments.[109]

Although the text bears witness to contacts with Judaism, it does not reveal any knowledge of the Hebrew, Aramaic, or Syriac languages. When it represents words or sentences in a Semitic language (see *APh* 2.18; *Martyrdom* 9 and 26), its renderings seem to originate from someone who may have heard Jews from Palestine speaking together but who had no understanding of what was being said. These examples of *lexeis barbarikai* serve as exotic examples rather than real information.[110]

Readers of the *Acts of Philip* will notice that some scenes are practically pure dialogue. We might wonder whether these episodes could not have been read by several voices or even have been performed on a stage. As Christians were opposed to the theater (see the attacks presented in many of John Chrysostom's sermons), these dialogues probably do not reflect an actual Christian production for the stage but a hopeful and permissible substitution to a theatrical performance.[111]

---

[108] On the popular character of this literature, see A. J. Festugière, *La révélation d'Hermès Trismégiste* (4 vols.; Paris: Les Belles Lettres, 1949–1954), 4:238. I thank Éric Junod who helped me find this reference.

[109] See note 84 above; Amsler, *Acta Philippi: Commentarius*, 156–71.

[110] See the note by Frédéric Amsler in Amsler, Bovon, and Bouvier, *Actes de l'apôtre Philippe*, 117–18 n. 111.

[111] On the status of theater at Byzantium, see Louis Bréhier, "Les miniatures des 'Homélies' du moine Jacques et le théâtre religieux à Byzance," in *Académie des inscriptions et belles-lettres* (Commission de la Fondation Piot. Monuments et mémoires 24; Paris, 1920), 101–28; George La Piana, "The Byzantine Theater," *Speculum* 11 (1936): 171–211.

CONCLUSION

Acts of Philip 1–7 is perhaps the merging of several independent tales originally connected with Philip the evangelist (Acts 6:1-6). *Acts of Philip* 8 through the *Martyrdom* recounts the missionary journey and the martyrdom of the apostle Philip. For the final author there is only one Christian leader with the name of Philip.[112] His companion from the New Testament lists of the Twelve, Bartholomew, and his sister, Mariamne, probably Mary Magdalene, accompany him. Two animals, a kid goat and a leopard, both symbols of universal redemption and an expression of the Christian victory over paganism, adopt Christian behavior and join the apostolic team on its missionary trip. The presence of a woman as a member of the apostolic team suits the church community of the author and his audience, a fourth-century ascetical group condemned by the Cappadocian Fathers and the church's decision at the Synod of Gangra (ca. 360 C.E.). The participation of tamed animals reflects this marginal community's belief in a redemption that embraces the whole creation.

The narrative is composed like those of other noncanonical Acts of the apostles, providing a sequence, numbered like in the *Acts of Thomas*, of individual acts of power and piety that demonstrate the strength and radiance of the Christian message over other cults—Jewish, Greek, and Anatolian religions—and over human sin, demonic forces, disease, and death. The model of these Acts of individual apostles is not the canonical book of Acts but the Gospels, with their concentration on Jesus as a singular religious hero and his passion narrative.[113]

The companionship of Mariamne and Bartholomew with Philip is a distinguishing difference between this text and most ancient apocryphal Acts of the apostles, such as the *Acts of John* and the *Acts of Andrew*. It brings the *Acts of Philip* closer to the "second wave" of noncanonical Acts (like the *Acts of Peter and Paul* or the *Acts of Andrew and Matthias*). This peculiarity provides a clue to the chronology of the text. The fourth century C.E. seems to be the most probable date of composition since this period also witnesses the condemnation of the encratite

---

[112] On Matthews' opinion, see note 35 above.

[113] See François Bovon, "La vie des apôtres, traditions bibliques et narrations apocryphes," in *Les Actes apocryphes des apôtres. Christianisme et monde païen* (Publications de la Faculté de théologie de l'Université de Genève 4; Geneva: Labor et Fides, 1981), 141–58, esp. 151–52.

communities of Asia Minor, apotactites and apostolics, by synods and Church Fathers. But the passages of higher literary level, most of them being prayers, are probably older and may be quoted from earlier sources by the authors of the *Acts of Philip*.

* * *

The following translation is based on the critical edition in the Corpus Christianorum: Series Apocryphorum 11, which utilizes several manuscripts, none of which is complete. In most cases the principal manuscript we follow is *Xenophontos 32*, though we depart from it for the *Martyrdom*.[114] In those cases where the text is not extant in *Xenophontos 32*, we indicate in the notes which manuscript is being utilized. But we do not signal all of the minor decisions made by the editors of the Greek text. Thus when the editors supply a missing definite article, signaled by its appearance within angle brackets in the critical text (e.g., <τοὺς> at *APh* 5.20, line 9), we simply translate "the" without the brackets. The reader is referred to the critical edition for the identification of such instances. Similarly on several occasions we add a word or two in the translation for clarification, normally without mention. We provide a minimal number of footnotes, both to allow the translation to speak for itself and so as not simply to duplicate much of the information already available. In this respect readers are urged to consult the following: François Bovon and Bertrand Bouvier's footnotes in the critical edition (along with the *apparatus biblicus* and the *apparatus fontium*); Frédéric Amsler's detailed interpretation in his commentary volume (CCSA 12), his footnotes in the volume of the series Apocryphes, and his footnotes in the volume of the Pléiade. Full bibliography on the *Acts of Philip* is available in Bovon, ANRW; in Amsler's commentary; in Matthews' *Philip: Apostle and Evangelist*; in Bovon, *New Testament and Christian Apocrypha*; and at the end of this volume, pp. 109–14.

---

[114] See p. 94 note 71 below.

TRANSLATION OF THE *ACTS OF PHILIP*

The First Act of the Holy Apostle Philip
When, Going Forth from Galilee, He Raised the Dead Man

Xenophontos 32 (A)

1. When Philip the apostle went forth from Galilee, a widow was carrying out for burial her only child, who was all she had. Now the apostle was very distressed in his soul when he saw the poor old woman tearing out her hair and disfiguring her face. He said to her: "What religion was your son practicing when he died so young?"

She replied: "Pardon me, I beg you, and do not interrogate me. For my heart has been cut in two, my voice given out, and I am unable to tell you the whole story. As one who has never wronged the gods, allow me to mourn this one not to be named, even though he is my son. I used to sacrifice daily—not a few offerings to Ares; spending quite lavishly on Apollo; for Hermes I have nearly broken my soul; I have sacrificed calves to Artemis; I brought a wreath to Zeus; I have offered goats for whole burnt-offerings to Athena; in a word, for as many gods as there are, I brought gifts to all, even to the Sun itself and to the Moon. Yet I believe that they have fallen asleep as regards me; I have cried out so much, but they have not heard me. Finally, constrained by necessity, I found a man who said he was a seer, and he said to me: 'For what reason, mother, do you wish me to practice my divination?' But he proved to be in no way unlike the gods, for everything he predicted to me was false. So divinations were useless to me and the gods worthless and blind. Indeed, is it possible that even I myself am like these impostors to whom I lost my goods, attending to worthless idols? I have lost my soul, and with it my money. For whoever worships idols or consults an oracle is cursed. Woe is me, from whom will I demand my money back, which I lost in vain by offering to idols and seers? I have despised the Christians; and now I have lost my son, who was all I had."

2. The apostle said: "You have not suffered anything strange, mother, having been deceived in such a way by the enemy who destroys souls; for this is how the devil deceives people and they fall short of eternal life. But as for you, stop mourning, for now I will raise your child by the power of my God Jesus Christ, who was crucified, buried, rose from the dead, and rules forever—whoever believes in him receives life eternal."

The old woman said: "May the things being said to me [. . .][1] of salvation, stranger, and as you are truly an apostle of God, help me in my old age, which has gone badly. While I suffered such evils, I prayed that I might die but I was not heard. Perhaps rather it is profitable not to marry or even not to eat any of those things that afterward agitate the body, wine and meat, but rather to eat bread and water, and avoid grief, many evils, and bitter suffering."

3. The apostle said to her: "Truly, mother, you do not utter this from yourself, but already the Savior speaks through you about purity. And what do you think about purity? Because God associates with purity itself,[2] and it creates much jealousy among people. For since they are not able to be pure or to drink water alone, they are eager to allege anything falsely against those who lead their lives purely. Therefore, God has blessed the latter. For God said: 'Blessed are you when people speak every lie against you. Rejoice and be glad, because your reward is great in the heavens, and on earth you will be able to silence demons without being anxious, since you have as a father Jesus, the crucified.'" After the apostle said these things, the old woman replied: "I believe in Jesus and in holy virginity."

---

[1] Not more than three words missing.

[2] The "purity" referred to here is not only moral but mystical since it facilitates communication with the divine. See the claim at 4.1 that "purity sees God."

4. Then the apostle drew near to the corpse and said: "Arise, young man, Jesus raises you for his own glory." And immediately he got up as if from sleep, and after looking straight at Saint Philip, he said: "How did the light of this man come into this place and raise me even though I had died—with such haste an angel of God came and opened the prison of judgment, where I had already been shut in—and how did I observe the torments and the punishments?

5. "I saw a woman resembling a dragon, and her hands like the tongues of serpents were whipping about, and she was holding a fiery rake and driving human souls into a chasm of fire. And I asked the angel: 'Who is this woman?' And he said to me: 'This woman incites people so that they might speak falsely about and laugh at the faithful; she incites them to say that Christ is a deceiver, and so leads them into this chasm. For by her insinuations she causes them to slander one to the other, and once she drives them with her rake, those whom she had deceived to engage in frivolous talk, in this way they have gone forward into damnation.

6. "Soon afterward I saw a man who was in an infernal pit whose teeth were grinding together in misery, and an angel stood by him with a sword of fire, and the man was being violently tortured without mercy. And I approached the angel to ask him to grant the man one hour of relief. And the angel said to me: 'Ask him what he did.' So I said to the one who was in the pit: 'What did you do to deserve this?' And he said to me: 'I tyrannized many and I beat bishops and priests,[3] and I spoke lies about them. I realize within myself that I deserve no mercy, so leave me to be tortured, for no one can escape the notice of God.' Now a leaden mass of about two hundred pounds hung down from him (for I even learned the weight) and in this way the poor man was being tortured. And I said to him: 'Why did you do those things?' He said to me: 'If I had known about these tortures, I would not be suffering in this way. For I assumed that there was no judgment after death, and so since I had such worthless thoughts, I am receiving what is fitting for the things that I did.'

7. "And again when I went on from there I saw a very young man, and the blades of his ribs were visible and he was lying on a bed of hot coals, and the filth flowing from his flesh turned into fiery serpents that leapt up and devoured him, and his punishment was incessant. And I said to

---

[3] The Greek word here is πρεσβύτερος, lit. "elder."

him: 'How awful for you, wretched man.' He said to me: 'If anyone does not listen to the warnings, all this happens to him. As for me, my tongue brought about my ruin, since I respected neither father nor mother nor priests; and moreover I insulted a most pious virgin, for I said that she was not a virgin, but that she was sinning. And this reproach came out of my mouth like fire, because I made her blush, in order that all who observed it might disdain her. I made her swear by the judge who judges the living and the dead. Yet instead I was found to be a perjurer, but she also appealed to God at the altar against me, and her curse upon me has come to pass. And her curse has not only hurt me, but also all of my relatives; for since they imitated me, they were judged, both the living and the dead. For this reason I am being punished, because I dishonored a virgin.' I said to him: 'Why did you do such things?' But he said to me: 'Speak to me no more, for I understand that there is no relief for me, because the hot coals are flaming up around me and the fiery serpents bite me more and more and I am being cruelly tortured.' And I was weeping and said: 'I pray, lead me away to the eunuchs and the virgins so I can ask repeatedly that they might grant relief to him, because he is being fearfully tortured.'

8. "And the archangel Michael met me with the key of fire and said to me: 'You can ask neither eunuchs nor virgins, for another is the one who judges. So if someone sins, he receives no mercy, and in the same way whoever makes false accusations receives no mercy, even if later he gives away his possessions to others, it avails nothing. And just as he made the lie known to everyone, so too his condemnation is made known to all. For whoever has lied against purity receives no mercy—neither this one, nor the hypocrite, nor the contentious, nor the liars, nor those who delight in hearing a wicked lie, because it is written: "If you make a false accusation and you do not correct it, you will be subject to the same tortures." In the same way everyone who conceals a sin receives no mercy.

9. "Next I saw some people who were taking balls of fire and throwing them at one another, and I said: 'Mercy, God have mercy, what is this?' And they said to me: 'We spoke much evil about the righteous and those leading lives in purity, saying that this one, or this one, or that one sinned. And since we had nothing true to say, we ran in vain and practiced in drunkenness the way of the lie. This is why we are attacking one another with balls and spits of fire.' And I said: 'The judgment of God is just.'

10. "When I went on from there, I saw a bald man and burning coals were being poured upon his head. And as he was being burned he was crying out, holding his head with both hands. And wherever he went an angel followed him with a ladle in his hand overflowing with globules of fire. And he held the ladle above him and let it drip down upon his head. So I asked him, saying: 'And you, what did you do?'—because the angel was not to be seen, for his punishment came about as though by the wind. And that one said to me: 'Wine has brought this upon me, for when I was drunk I frequently slandered bishops, priests, eunuchs, and virgins. For I used to reproach them as licentious people, and I began to recite lyrics against them. So just as I used to speak words against their heads, thus I receive back in turn as much against my head. And just as I concocted lyrics about them, so now I receive my due reward and am letting loose this scream as I am being burned, wailing for my poor head.' And as I beheld that poor man, his punishment seemed unjust to me, because he was old and advanced in years, and I said: 'I beg you,[4] show me where the virgins are.' And they said to me: 'You cannot see them, unless when you go back to the world you receive baptism and obtain purity for yourself. You can see neither eunuch, nor virgin, nor one made pure by repentance. Therefore, leave this unfortunate man to be punished, for it is not necessary for the servants of God †. . .†[5] to think upon or speak about.' And when I heard that they spoke rightly, I said: 'Suffer, wretched man, what is coming down upon your head.' And when I said this, I left him to his torment. And as I was about to withdraw, he cried out: 'If you can do anything, help me.' And I said: 'I beg you,[6] at least show me the place of the virgins.'

11. "And as I was going about and searching, even though no one was guiding me, the archangel Michael met me and said to me: 'Why do you labor in vain? Do you not know that a curse was hurled with bitterness against the baldheaded man while he was alive,[7] and there is no mercy, because the poor man was badly deceived by wine? For much wine brings about whispered gossip, anger, jealousy, hypocrisy,

---

[4] It is not clear to whom the young man refers with this second-person plural pronoun since in the previous scenes his guide was a single angel (the archangel Michael according to 1.8).

[5] The precise meaning of the two verbs is not clear because of a lacuna of about eleven letters.

[6] Another second-person plural pronoun (see note 4).

[7] Lit., "in the world."

licentiousness, arrogance, and everything that is like them. For the ladle also waits for them, and especially idolaters and augurs and diviners and sorcerers and magicians, and the moving ladle is whirling around them.' And I said: 'I'm going away from here. For someone is calling me to depart to the world and I don't know who it is.' And the chief angel Michael said to me: 'I have been authorized to release you. It remains for you then to hasten toward the one who is summoning you. Yet if you, although you are free from these torments, wish to go over and see the punishments, how many days are enough for you?'[8]

12. "When I heard this I was making haste to get away, and as I was going out I saw beside the gate a man and a woman; and the great dog named Cerberus, who has three mouths, was secured at the gate with chains of fire; and he was gnawing on the man and the woman and he was holding their livers with his feet. And these two as half-dead were crying out: 'Have mercy on us, help us.' But no one was helping them. And I went to restrain the dog, but Michael said to me: 'Leave it be, because these also blasphemed against male and female priests, eunuchs, deacons, deaconesses, and virgins with lies about debauchery and adultery. And since those defamed were greatly disturbed, they turned to me, Michael, and to Raphael, and to Oriel, and we gave the blasphemers as food to this dog until the great day of judgment.' And I said, 'Chief angel Michael, torture them further.' Then he said to me: 'There is neither mercy for them, nor for those who wish to imitate them, because †. . .†.[9] And not only here, but also while they are still alive I will show them many things, unless they wish to repent. For I will bring upon them demons, sorrows, and afflictions; I will send them despotic men who will inflict on them much evil.' Then I hastened to go to the one who had summoned me and said to myself: 'When I depart from here I will relate these things to those in the world, because there is much chastisement here.'

13. "After I exited the gate,[10] I beheld an altar, and the celebrants of the altar were jealous men and from one to the other were steeped in hypocrisy. And I said: 'How many torments I have seen on account

---

[8] That is, such a tour of the place of torment could go on for quite some time.

[9] There are about twenty-five letters, approximately three words, between the daggers whose sense is not clear.

[10] The location here, apparently outside of hell, is not clear; some liminal border is crossed at "the gate."

of them, and look how much they do in hypocrisy.' And the chief angel Michael said to me: 'Stay and see that these also will undergo punishment. For no one receives preferential treatment from God. Indeed the jealous person or hypocrite or envious one or irascible person or the one who mistreats inopportunely and the one who incites disorder and the one who judges unjustly, these have toiled there.

"As I moved on from there I beheld an immense throne, the nature of which I cannot describe. It was composed of something like flowers. And I perceived something like thunder coming out from the throne and it was summoning the celebrants of the altar. And it found reasons for many condemnations against them, including drunkenness and silly talk, and it was saying to them: 'Is it not written: "If anyone throws about a careless word, that person will be deserving of judgment"? I am not treating you unjustly, rather you accuse yourselves.' To another it was saying: 'It is written for you: "Do not be angry." But when you mistreated out of anger you delivered a whipping. See, you have sinned against another through slander.' To another it said: 'Do you not find in scripture: "Whatever you hate, do not do to another"? Yet you accuse yourself, for although you were reading, you did not understand.' The others were groaning and gloomy. And the chief angel Michael was saying to them: 'As many of you as wish to be pious, beware of the wolf. For outwardly he appears to be a sheep, but inwardly he is a savage wolf.' And he told them: 'Unless you convert, you will receive no mercy.'

14. "I myself saw these things, Philip, servant of God, and my soul is very troubled; for I am afraid that the deceiving devil may actually be playing with me and will yet drag me into those punishments."

15. Philip said: "What, then, have you seen? What you beheld is insignificant and limited. As for you, protect yourself and receive the holy washing. Just as those there have told you, unless you keep yourself spotless, you will fall into those punishments. Therefore, child, you have no need of a teacher, since you have seen once for all the punishments for sins. If then you should fight well, you will become forever a patron for many."

16. The young man said: "Permit me, apostle of God, to say something; for I have remembered something." The apostle said: "Speak, child." And the boy said: "As I was coming into this solidly constructed[11]

---

[11] This verb, which bears a double prepositional prefix (διασυγκείμενον), is otherwise unattested. Note that the manuscript has "ν" for "γ."

world, I beheld two banished men whose hands were bound behind their backs and they were being tortured in a frying pan. And there was nearby a vessel full of lead which was bubbling, and their guard forced them [. . .][12] and they drank the lead, and on the outside they were burning with fire and on the inside from the lead. And I asked for what reason they were being tormented like this, and the angel said to me: 'These did much evil on earth; indeed they condemned innocent people, treated them shamefully, and despised them, having considered themselves to be righteous. They embittered the servants of God, saying: "What can these people do to us?" So they were tyrannizing, haughty, slandering, taking part one with the other whether in strong drink or in robbery of the poor and in greed, attaching themselves to folly they have found punishment, being pained also by the wealth left on earth. These here are being fried even while their former pleasure remains in the world. They are drinking bubbling lead because they were intoxicated with all evils. For whatever a person does from self-interest, it will return to him here, since he idly played the fool with his reckless tongue.'

17. "After I beheld these things I was snatched away from there by a wind and I came here, in order that after being raised by you I might describe all this. Therefore, if anyone wishes to receive mercy, he will keep away from all these evil sins; if anyone believes in God, that one will be blessed; and if anyone confesses the beloved Christ, that one will be glorified. And the way of the righteous, I have seen that it leads by a different route into the place of refreshment, because they believed in Jesus while they were alive."

18. And so the boy who was raised from the dead together with his mother believed fervently, and consequently they converted many. And when these received baptism through them, they were glorifying God. And when they had given abundant provisions for the road to the apostle, they departed, having believed in Christ. But the young man followed the apostle, exalting in himself at the wonders that were being done by him every day. And they were all glorifying God, amen.

---

[12] The major portion of the line has been erased.

The Second Act of the Holy Apostle Philip
In Hellas of the Athenians

PVXK (A)

1. Now it happened when Philip entered into the city of the Athenians, called Hellas, three hundred philosophers gathered before him and said: "Since we have come, let us hear what his wisdom is; for they say with respect to the sages of Asia that it is great." For they supposed Philip to be a philosopher, since[13] he was traveling in the guise of a hermit,[14] and they did not know that he was an apostle of Christ. For the clothing that Jesus gave to the apostles was only a short tunic and a wrap. Accordingly Philip was going around in this manner. So for this reason when the philosophers of Hellas saw him, they were frightened. Then they gathered together in one place and said to each other: "Come, let us consult our books, lest this stranger vanquish us and dishonor us."

2. So after they did this, they gathered at the same spot and said to Philip: "We have teachings of our fathers which are sufficient for our philosophizing. But if you have something new, stranger, show it to us with boldness, holding nothing back.[15] For we have no other need than to listen to something novel."

3. Philip answered and said to them: "Gentlemen, philosophers of Hellas, if you wish to hear some novel thing and you are longing for something new, you ought to cast off from yourselves the mind of the old human being. As my Lord said: 'It is not possible to put new wine into old wineskins, since the wineskin bursts and the wine pours out and the wineskin is ruined. Rather, one puts new wine into new wineskins, so that both may be preserved.' But the Lord said these things in parables, teaching us by his holy wisdom that many will love the new wine without possessing new wineskins. Now then, I love you, men of Hellas, and I bless you since you have said 'we love what is novel.' For

---

[13] *Xenophontos 32* (A) breaks off here in the middle of the word "since" (ἐπει|[. . .]). The manuscripts containing the following text are: P = *Parisinus graecus 881*; V = *Vaticanus graecus 824*; X = *Vaticanus graecus 866*; and K = *Ambrosianus graecus 405*.

[14] The term ἀποτακτικός is known from the fourth century on in Christian literature in connection with monks and heretical groups. Such people may have intended to imitate philosophical (esp. Cynic) garb.

[15] The adverb ἀφθόνως has a range of meaning from "without envy" to "abundantly."

my Lord brought really fresh and new teaching into the world so that he might wipe away all worldly instruction."

4. The philosophers said: "Who is the one you are calling your Lord?" Philip said: "My Lord is Jesus, who is in heaven." And they said to him: "Show him to us with insight and without envy so that we also might believe." So Philip said: "The Lord I am going to make known to you is far above every name; it is like no other.[16] But I am only saying this because just as you have said, 'do not be envious of us,' may it never be that I should be envious of you. But rather with great exaltation and joy I have to reveal that name to you. For I have no other task in this world except such proclamation. For when my Lord came into this world, he chose us who were twelve in number, having filled us with the Holy Spirit from his light. He enabled us to make known who he is, and he commanded us to preach the good news of the salvation issuing from him to everyone, because there is not another name named from heaven except this one. For this reason I myself have come to you to give you full assurance not in word only but also by demonstration of wondrous deeds, in the name of my Lord Jesus Christ."

5. When the philosophers heard these things, they said to Philip: "This name that we have now heard from you we have never found in the books of our fathers. So how then can we go about confirming your word?" Moreover, when they continued they said to him: "Allow us three days so that we may confer with one another about this name, for it is no small matter if we move toward this and desert our ancestral religion." Philip said to them: "Deliberate as you wish, for it is not a deceitful thing that I am doing."

6. So when the three hundred philosophers gathered themselves together, they spoke with one another, saying: "Recognize that this man has brought a strange philosophy, and the words spoken by him bring us into an ecstasy. So what should we do about him or about the name of the one called Jesus, whom he says is the king of the ages?" Moreover, they said to one another: "Perhaps we ourselves are not capable of debating with him, but only the high priest of the Jews. Therefore, if it seems proper, let us send for him, that he might oppose this stranger and that we might learn accurately about the name he preaches."

---

[16] For parallels to the construction here in both form and content, see Gal 1:7; Acts 4:12; and Heb 1:4.

7. So they wrote to Jerusalem in the following manner: "The philosophers of Hellas to Ananias, the great high priest of the Jews in Jerusalem, greetings. Since there is great peace between you and us at all times, and since you know we Athenians love to philosophize, a stranger named Philip came to Hellas and, simply put, disturbed us very much by his words and his extraordinary acts of power. He introduces a glorious name, Jesus, declaring himself to be a disciple of that one. He also does wonders which we are writing to you about. Namely, he has cast out demons that have chronically afflicted people, makes the deaf hear, the blind regain their sight, and what is even more wondrous, which it would be proper to make known first, he has raised people who had completed the allotment of their lives and had died. His fame has spread through all of Hellas and Macedonia, and numerous are those who come to him from the surrounding cities bringing those who suffer with various diseases, and he cures all of them by the name of Jesus. For this reason, therefore, sparing no delay, come to us, so that you yourself may inform us what the name that he teaches, Jesus, means. For this reason we have sent you this letter, high priest."

8. Now when the high priest received the letter and read it, he was filled with great anger and he tore his garments and said: "Has that deceiver also gone on to Athens among the philosophers to beguile them?" Then Mansemat,[17] that is Satan, entered secretly into Ananias and filled him with rage and anger. And he said: "If I allow that Philip and those with him to live, the law will be totally destroyed and their teaching will probably fill the whole earth." The high priest entered his house with the teachers of the law and the Pharisees, and they conferred with one another, saying: "What should we do about these things?"[18] And they said to the high priest: "Ananias, rise up and arm five hundred strong men from the people for yourself and go to Athens, and you will do away with Philip altogether and thus you will overthrow his teaching."

9. And so clothed with the high priestly garment, Ananias arrived in Hellas with great pomp with the five hundred men. Now Philip was in the house of a leading citizen of the city with the brothers and sisters who had believed. Then the high priest and those with him as well as the three hundred philosophers came to the porch of the house in which Philip was staying. Philip was informed that they stood outside; so he

---

[17] Cf. Mastema in *Jubilees* 10:8.
[18] Or, "these people."

rose and went out. And when the high priest saw him, he said to him: "Philip, you sorcerer and magician, I recognize you, because in Jerusalem your Lord, the deceiver, named you Son of Thunder.[19] Was not all of Judea enough for you that you have even come here to beguile the Athenian philosophers?" Philip said: "Ananias, would that your veil of unbelief be removed from your heart so that you might understand my words and learn from them whether the deceiver is me or you."

10. When Ananias heard this he said to Philip: "I will respond to everything." Philip said: "Speak." The high priest said: "People of Hellas, this Philip believes in a man called Jesus, who was born among us, who also taught this heresy, disregarded both the law and the temple, and abolished both Sabbath observation and the purification rites of Moses as well as new moon observances, because he said these had not been instituted by God. When we saw that he was destroying the law in this way, we rebelled and crucified him so that his teaching might not spread. For he enrolled a great number under his command, and he gave a bad witness: to eat everything without distinction and to mingle with pagans. And having delivered up this man we murdered him, and we buried him in a tomb. Then when these disciples of his had stolen him, they proclaimed everywhere that he had been raised from the dead, and they led a great number astray when they confessed him to be at the right hand of God in heaven. But they themselves are circumcised even as we are. So we persecuted them, since they began to do many miracles in Jerusalem by the name of Jesus. So having been driven out from Jerusalem they travel about throughout the world deceiving everyone with the magic of that Jesus, as even now this Philip has come to you to deceive you with the same cunning. But I will bring this one back with me to Jerusalem, because Archelaus the king is also seeking him in order to kill him."

11. When the crowd that had been standing there heard these things, those who had been established in the faith were neither shaken nor doubtful, for they knew that Philip would prevail with the glory of Jesus. Then Philip defended himself by the power of Christ with great boldness, exalting and saying: "Athenians and those who are philosophers among you, I came to you not with words to teach but with a demonstration of wonders, which also in part perhaps you have seen

---

[19] In Mark 3:17 Jesus designates James and John, the sons of Zebedee, "Sons of Thunder."

being accomplished by me in that name which this high priest rejects. Therefore, behold, I will call out to my God and I will teach you, and you yourselves test the words of both of us."

12. After the high priest heard this, he ran up to Philip intending to whip him. But at that moment his hand withered and his eyes were blinded. And in the same way the five hundred with him were themselves also blinded. And they were insulting and cursing the high priest, saying: "When we came out of Jerusalem, we were saying to you: 'Restrain yourself, for as human beings we cannot fight with God.' But we beseech you, Philip, apostle of the God of Jesus, give us the light that comes through him, so that we also may truly be his servants."

13. When Philip saw what had happened, he said: "O weak nature, which raises itself against us, then immediately utterly abases itself; O bitter sea, which stirs up its waves against us and thinks to frighten us, only to see the waves settle in itself. Now, then, our good steward, Jesus, the holy light, you have not disregarded us altogether as we cried out above to you in all good works, but you came to perfect them through us. Now then, come, Lord Jesus, expose the madness of these people."

14. The high priest said to Philip: "You don't think to convert us from the traditions of our fathers and the God of the wilderness and the manna and Moses, and expect us to follow the Nazarene Jesus, do you?" Then Philip said to him: "Look, I will pray to my God so that he may come and reveal himself before you and the five hundred and before everyone here; for when you repent, perhaps you will believe. But if you persist in unbelief to the end, an incredible event will come upon you which will be spoken about for countless generations, namely, that you will descend alive below into Hades before all those who see you, because you still remain in your unbelief and because you seek to turn this crowd away from true life." Then Philip prayed, saying: "Holy Father of your holy Son Jesus Christ, you who have granted me the grace of believing in him. Send your beloved Son Jesus Christ to reprove the unbelieving high priest, so that your name may be glorified in the beloved Christ."

15. And while Philip was still crying out these things, suddenly the heavens opened and Jesus appeared, descending in the rarest glory and lightning; and his face was shining seven times brighter than the sun and his garments were whiter than snow. And all the idols of Athens suddenly fell to the ground and all were broken in pieces, and the demons in them were fleeing, crying out: "See, we are fleeing because of Jesus,

the Son of God, who has appeared in the city." Then Philip said to the high priest: "Do you hear the demons crying out because of the one who has appeared, and do you refuse to believe before the one who is present that he himself is the Lord of all?" The high priest said: "I myself have no other God except the one who gave the manna in the wilderness."

16. Now while Jesus was ascending into heaven, a strong earthquake occurred so that the place upon which they had been standing was split open. And the crowds ran and were lying down at the apostle's feet screaming: "Have mercy on us, Man of God." Likewise also the five hundred men themselves cried out in turn: "Have mercy on us, Philip, so that we may see you and through you the torch of life, Jesus. Because we were also saying to this unbelieving priest that we being 'sinful people cannot fight with God.'"

17. Then Philip said: "Envy is not in us, on the contrary the grace of Christ will make you see again. But first I will make your high priest see again so that on this basis you may believe all the more." And a voice came out of heaven to Philip: "Philip, formerly son of thunder, but now of gentleness, whatever you ask my father, he will do it for you." The entire crowd was awestruck at the voice, for its sound was louder than thunder. Then Philip said to the high priest: "In the name of the power of the voice of my Lord Jesus, see again, Ananias." And immediately he recovered his sight, and after he looked around he said: "O, how effective is the magic of Jesus. For this Philip blinded me with one word, and again with one word he made me regain my sight." "What then," said Philip. "Do you believe in Jesus?" The high priest said: "You don't think you can enchant me and persuade me, do you?" When the five hundred who were with him heard that their high priest having regained his sight was still unbelieving, they were saying to those standing round: "Implore Philip that he might make us see again that we might do away with this unbelieving high priest."

18. Philip said: "Do not defend yourselves by evil means." And he said to the high priest: "A sign will come upon you, something great." He said to Philip: "I know that you are a sorcerer and a disciple of Jesus; you are not going to enchant me." But the apostle said to Jesus: "*Zavarthan, savathavat, vramanouch*, come quickly." And immediately the earth was split open below the place where Ananias was and it swallowed him to his knees. And Ananias cried out: "O, surely this is great trickery, that the earth has split itself open after Philip threatened and adjured it in Hebrew. And it holds me up to my knees, and some creatures pull at

me by the heels as if with hooks toward the world below so that I will believe Philip. But he cannot persuade me, for I am acquainted with his magic tricks from Jerusalem."

19. Philip was angered and said: "O earth, take hold of him up to the navel." And immediately he was pulled down. And he was saying: "My one foot is being frozen from below, but the other is being scorched terribly. Yet I will not be defeated, Philip, by your magic. Even though I am being badly tormented from below, I do not believe at all." The crowds wanted to stone him, but Philip said: "Don't be like this, for what has happened up to now, his having been swallowed up to the navel, happened so that salvation might come to your souls. Because he was almost going to draw you by his evil words toward unbelief. Yet if he himself would repent, I would bring him up out of the earth for the salvation of his soul. But perhaps he is not worthy of salvation. Therefore, if he persists in unbelief, you will see him being dragged down below into the abyss, unless the Lord is about to raise up those in Hades so that they might confess that Jesus is Lord. For on that day every tongue will confess that Jesus is Lord, and that there is one glory of the Father and the Son with the Holy Spirit forever."

20. After Philip said these things he stretched out his right hand and made a gesture in the air over the five hundred men in the name of Jesus. And their eyes were opened and they all sang praises to God with one voice, saying: "Blessed are you, Jesus Christ, God of Philip, because you have driven away our blindness and your light has been established in us, and we have come to know the gospel." And Philip was rejoicing at their words more and more, because in this way they were being strengthened in the faith. Then after these things Philip turned toward the high priest and said: "You too, confess with a clean heart that Jesus is Lord, so that you may be saved like these who came with you." But the high priest was laughing at Philip and persisting in unbelief. 21. Accordingly when Philip saw that he was persisting in unbelief, he looked at him and he said to the earth: "Open your mouth and swallow him up to his neck in front of those who believe in Christ Jesus." And at that moment the earth opened its mouth and received him as far as his neck.

22. Now while the crowds were talking among themselves on account of the wonders that had taken place, one of the city fathers came, crying out and saying: "Blessed apostle, a demon has come upon my son, and he called out, saying to me: 'Since you, being a city father, have permitted a stranger to enter into our city, who has destroyed our

rites and our sacrifices, what should I do to you except kill this your only son?' And after he said these things he suffocated my son. Now then, I beg you, apostle of Christ, do not allow my joy to be turned into grief, because I too have believed in your words."

23. When the apostle heard these things, he said: "I am astonished by the power of the demons, because it is at work in every place and it dares to attack those over whom it has no control; so now they have tempted you, wishing to make you fall." And he said to the man: "Bring your son to me, and I will give him back to you alive through my Christ." And he ran off rejoicing to fetch his son. And when he drew near to his house, he cried out, saying: "My son, you see, I have come to you to take you to the apostle, who will grant you to me alive." And he commanded his servants to carry the bed. Now the young man was twenty-three years old. When Philip saw him, he was deeply troubled, and he turned to the high priest and said to him: "This has happened on account of your foolishness. If, then, I raise him, will you finally believe?" And he said: "I know your[20] magic, that you will raise him; but I will not believe you." Then, being provoked to anger, Philip said: "A curse on you! Depart now entirely into the abyss below in front of all these people." And at that moment he descended alive into Hades. The high priestly garment, however, sailed away from him. And this is why from that day on no one knows what became of the priestly garment. And turning around the apostle prayed for the young man, expelled the demon from him, raised him up, and delivered him alive to his father.

24. When the crowds saw these things, they cried out: "There is one God, the God of Philip, who rebuked the unbelief of the high priest, expelled the demon from the young man, and raised him from the dead." Now when the five hundred men saw the high priest plunged into the abyss and the other marvels, they beseeched the apostle, and he gave them the seal in Christ.

Now Philip stayed in Athens for two years. And after he built a church, he appointed a bishop and a priest. And thus he departed for Parthia, preaching the gospel of Christ. To him be glory forever, amen.

---

[20] Here the second-person plural form is followed by singular forms. "I know your [pl.] magic, that you [s.] will raise him. . . ."

The Third Act of the Holy Apostle Philip
In Parthia

Xenophontos 32 (A)

1. When Philip, the apostle of Christ, arrived in the realm of Parthia, suddenly he encountered in a certain city Peter, the apostle of Christ, along with the other disciples with him, as well as some women who were imitating the male faith. Philip said to Peter and those with him: "I beg you, inspired ones, I beg you who have received the crown of Christ in the apostolic order, strengthen me also, so that when I depart I might preach the gospel and be numbered among you in your glory in the heavens and in the zeal, delight, mortification of the flesh, and courageous heart of those who are humble in continence. You yourselves have shown your zeal in line with your power. Therefore pray also now on my behalf, in order that I might preach the gospel when I depart and be numbered among those who have perfected their power." When Philip had said this they bent their knees on his behalf to the Lord, with the result that everyone rejoiced over him since Philip had sought in this way to perfect his apostleship and service.

2. Now the blessed John was there and he said to Philip: "My brother and my fellow apostle, if you too are making a distant journey, know that brother Andrew has traveled to Achaia and all of Thrace, and Thomas to India and the murderous cannibals, and Matthew to the unmerciful troglodytes, for their nature is savage. Yet the Lord will be with us. Therefore you, Philip, do not be hesitant, for Jesus is with you."

3. Now when Philip related in detail what had occurred at Athens, they glorified God. And Philip said: "I implore you, blessed John, and you, blessed Peter, pray on my behalf that I too might perfect my apostleship just as the Lord has entrusted it to me." And when they had prayed a great deal on his behalf, a voice was conveyed from heaven, saying: "Make haste, Philip! Look, my angel is with you and you should not be negligent." At that moment the blessed Philip went forth rejoicing exceedingly because he had been considered worthy of such a voice. And he took with him three loaves of bread and five staters, because he was traveling a long way. Now Jesus was walking with him in secret, strengthening him, so that the senses of the new human being were opened. And the Spirit of the Lord filled him with apologetic ability, because formerly he was quite unskilled in speech.

4. So Philip was rejoicing along the way when he recognized that he was not like he was the day before or previously. Being filled with the Holy Spirit by grace, he desired a vision of glory and he said: "Lord Jesus, write for me the words of this understanding. For if your harmonious care is with me, Jesus, since I am worthy of understanding just like my brothers, show yourself to me, you who are present in secret, by manifesting your glory, you who move souls fixed in the essence of death and re-create them in your wisdom; you who establish those who are shaken in the upbuilding of purity; you who have been suspended from the interior places. We ourselves listened in a worthy manner, in order that we might know the way. You who grant us good things in the goodness of the Father, Savior of the powerless, reveal yourself to me, the one who loves you. For I hope that I will see you also in heaven, you who are above the heavens. Let those who do not receive you see your glory. You who hear the hymn of the powers, hear me too, because I have loved you. You who search the hearts of the wise, but no one is able to search you out. You who grant power to the new root before all things, grant power also to me, because you are worthy of that day. Physician of our inner person, strengthen me also in your wisdom. One without beginning, you who are yourself the beginning of life, grant me friendship with your light. Unconquerable chariot, good tidings of the Father, carry my prayer up into the glory above. Lord of the archangels, be my Lord, for I am your servant. You who are the defense in the courts, grant also a defense to me so that you might be glorified in me, you who fill your storehouses[21] with understanding and give it to the faithful heart; you who enlighten the unenlightened so that the intelligent might see; immeasurable voice that comes from on high; you who establish us in your divinity and in your kindness; you who consider the one who is present and wait patiently for those who are ignorant of you. Garment of the Father, you have covered us with your inexpressible power, because we were naked before your coming. But when you came, your new salvation conquered our former fall. You yourself know what is in my heart, you who have granted good thoughts to those who are ignorant of you. Indeed, all the people do not know your glory. You are the virtue of knowledge that bears what is hidden to the light, you are the sprinkling that sprinkles our thanksgiving. Grant me the gift through your source

---

[21] In the phrase τοὺς θησαυροὺς αὐτοῦ, the term αὐτοῦ is used for the second person singular.

from the Father, which pours out and waters souls. You are our lawgiver and the one who calls us by your sweet voice. You who are one, both alone and many—Who will measure your name? You who are the one who is coming to us in all glory, listen to me, Jesus, in my prayer. For I know that I was not like this before these days, because you have surely remembered me and given me your understanding."

5. Now when Philip ended the prayer, suddenly a great plant appeared in the deserted place, and he ran and sat under the plant and ate bread. And when he looked up above he saw something like a great eagle perched there and its wings had been extended according to the form[22] of the true cross. So Philip said: "You, beautiful eagle with your wings extended, fly above and take up my petition, because I have been in grief of heart until the present moment, because the Savior has not appeared to me. For I notice about you that you are a chosen bird and that your beauty is not of this place."

6. When Philip turned this over in his heart, he said in the spirit: "Perhaps even now, Lord Jesus Christ, you are the one revealing yourself in this form, just as you have been accustomed to manifest yourself to the saints. For your glory is more beautiful on the lips of the righteous. Great is this form, the form in which I behold you. Yet how did you appear on this plant, Jesus, since you are exalted? And how did you endure being made humble, since you are the Lord? And how did you bear being called a servant? And how, since you are eternal, did you associate with birth? You were fixed on a cross in order that you might set us free from the nails, granting us unceasing, unshaded, ever-shining, nightless light.[23] And now as an eagle stretches out its wings you have become my shelter in the wilderness." 7. And when he bent his knees again, he was saying: "I worship you, Lord, because now I know that you have remembered me and have listened to me and have shown me your glory. For you are a just father and advocate and you save those who hope on you. My tongue is incapable of speaking what is in my heart about you. But you are the one who examines minds, who tests hearts, and who perceives designs. You are the Son and you are the Father and everything is in you, eternal life, the glory of the Father."

---

[22] The term here is τύπος; it also appears in paragraph 6, line 3.
[23] The words "granting us" and "light" in this sentence are necessary restorations by the editors of the Greek text. We ordinarily translate such restorations without notice.

8. Then Jesus said to Philip as though from the mouth of the eagle: "Listen, I blessed you in your prayer and I shall be stretched out over you in my glory. With regard to those who are ignorant of me, I will strengthen you by my light and I shall become strong in you and there will be great opportunities. I will be your guide in remote regions and you will walk in my footsteps and you will expose those without understanding. Be on guard against the one who lies in ambush, because he runs about seeking to trip others up and he darkens them with gloom. His way does not lead to success, but I will be your safe way. Be mindful in your understanding, because I will be your dry land when crossing over rivers, your heavenly helmsman at sea, and a haven from stormy weather on the open sea. I will neither be distant from you nor forsake you. For even now I am attending to Thomas in the Labyrinth, and I am also just now comforting John in Asia; I am sustaining Andrew in Achaia and praying together with your fellow apostles." 9. Philip said: "How then should I sing praises to your goodness, Lord? Because at first you were with us, Jesus, and many among us refused to believe in you. But when you were taken up, we did not realize that you would be going along with us in such a form. For when you hid yourself in the body, then you revealed yourself in the spirit. And since you were beside us, sweet and perfectly wise, you were coming to us secretly in understanding." The Lord said to him: "Rise, Philip; proceed. Look, I am with you."

10. Then Philip went by sea to the borders of the Candaceans, and he found there a ship about to sail for Azotus. And he said to the sailors: "Take me, you sailors, and bring me also to Azotus." And he agreed to give them four staters as a fare, and he went on board with them.

11. And when they had sailed some four hundred stadia,[24] a strong wind came up so that the ship was endangered. Then fierce locusts arrived on the wind and consequently harmed the men on the ship. 12. Philip arose and came onto the prow and said: "Who is the one who aroused this wind to produce its children to harm people by their savage nature?" And he cried out, saying: "O merciful Lord Jesus Christ, you who have revealed yourself to me and told me, 'If ever you call upon me, I will hear you.' Listen, I am calling upon you now because of this pressing danger." Now it was about midnight when he said these words. And he saw a shining signet in the form of the cross, for it was dark. Now the signet was giving off more and more light, so that the sailors also saw

---

[24] About fifty miles.

the brilliance of a light brighter than the sun. And the brightness that had come about in the middle of the sky illuminated the depths of the sea. And when the sea monsters and the fish and the beasts beheld this brilliance in the sea, they formed into a circle, did obeisance to the light, and cried out hymns in their language. And the sea was transformed by the majesty of the light, and the wind also ceased and the locusts died in the sea. "But we ourselves stood fast, rejoicing in the light, that it came to us."

13. When Philip responded, he said: "What kind of grace do we have to give in return for this grace and power? Human grace cannot attain to this glory, can it? Therefore rise and open your hearts in prayer without moving your lips with your words, because great is the glory that has appeared in all the world. Where then was this glory during that time, Jesus, when you were with us being laughed at and condemned like a man? The tax collectors of the world finally did not believe in you. So like a stranger who walks with us you have guided us by walking in your goodness, knowing what will come. Who can compare you to a begotten body? You did not appear to the world as the glory visible now, rather:

> You hid this glory until the naked should be transformed.
> You hid this glory until those desiring to know you should work hard.
> You hid this glory until they should see your glorious face.
> You hid this glory until those in ignorance should recognize you.
> You hid this glory until those who have sought you should find you.
> You hid this glory during the time in which you were about to be revealed.
> You hid this glory until your form manifested itself and it was known that it is not of this place.
> You hid this glory in order that the new person might know you in uprightness.
> You hid this glory until those who had fallen asleep might be awakened.
> You hid this glory until the sheep that were not scattered might know you.
> You hid this glory until those who had been close to perdition might turn back.
> You hid this glory until you manifested yourself to this people.
> You hid this glory until the heavenly eye that appeared to the world was revealed.

You hid this glory until silence resulted before your unutterable teaching.
You hid this glory until the inheritance was revealed in us.
You hid this glory when not even one of those who happened to be in the world was worthy of it.

But now, perhaps, since you have revealed yourself to these few, you have made known your glory."

14. As Philip spoke these words, the signet of light was in the sky and on the sea so that the winds and the sea were quiet—indeed the winds were no longer harsh—and the men who were on the ship and the sailors were amazed at such a manifestation of power. And it was a silence that nobody had ever witnessed. "Now for the greater part of the night, I, Philip, heard voices singing that cannot be compared to those from human lips. And after this ceased, then the heavens were opened to the heights and the signet was lifted up into heaven. And when day broke we were sitting on the ship remembering what had appeared to us; and the sun rose as though it were trembling, and we were unsettled,[25] staring into the air.

15. "When we came to ourselves, we had drawn near to the harbor of Azotus. When the ship was moored at the shore, the sailors were conversing about the glory that had appeared, saying: 'How troubled we were in our souls.' And when I had talked to them at length, I strengthened them in the Lord." Then Philip started to give the sailors the four-stater fare for his passage, and the sailors said to him: "Do not do this! For what we have seen is payment enough. And we believe that whenever we will be in danger while at sea, we will be saved by the signet that appeared. And how blessed will the city be on whose ground your feet will tread, and blessed are those who hear the word from your lips. We are truly blessed since you came on board our humble ship, because through you we were rescued from the harshness of the sea. And we will trust that our souls will be enlightened by the signet that appeared." And they ran up to the city, proclaiming about Philip and reporting as much as they had seen. And many believed and were glorifying God.

16. While this was happening, Philip went up to the city and stood before the gate. Now he was wearing a coat and a shoulder strap of fine

---

[25] We take the term μετέωρος metaphorically; used literally it can mean "raised from off the ground," "on the surface," "in midair," "high in the air," "on the high sea."

linen. When he had looked upon those standing around, he said: "You men who are with me, we must seek out our lodgings. For you ought to receive my words like gifts of the Most High. But let it not be a scandal for you to be in the foreign company of the Foreigner.[26] Wherefore I urge you to look upon the perfect stone that was neither placed nor hewn, which is precious, chosen, pointed, marvelous, God-bearing. Acknowledge him in your heart and in your soul.

17. "Heed the difference between the soul and the flesh. The purification of the soul is the Holy Spirit of immortality which looks to its own habitations, which Jesus has given. Continence of the flesh is rest for the soul seeking the lofty designation. Humiliation of the flesh is a gift for the soul. Understanding the flesh is wisdom for the soul. Almsgiving of the flesh[27] is anxiety-free upbuilding for the soul. Flesh that does not humiliate itself is a wound for the soul. If you receive the one who is able to save the weak, you will be saved. If you receive the one who is rich in heaven, he will enrich you. 18. I say this according to the type of the eagle. For when it begets its young it takes them up into the heights, and in their own language they call to their father: 'Our father, where are you taking us?' And he says, 'Children, your essence is in the heights and you have nothing to do with what is below. Do not fear flying into the heights, because there is one who carries you. Do not look at what is below, because there is an enemy who waits in ambush.' Now I say these things not about the nature of eagles alone, but also about all the birds. Let this example be sufficient for you. I say to you who are obedient to these things and are being lifted up to your own essence, hear the word and look up toward the essence above, being taught in your understanding so that you will be worthy of rebirth. Leave behind the odious character of this world, casting the anxiety of life upon the benefactor in heaven, and you will enjoy eternal luxury."

19. When many who were sick and weakened became healthy in that hour, they glorified the God Jesus being preached by Philip and they were growing in the faith as they were being baptized in the grace of Christ. To him be glory forever and ever, amen.

---

[26] We take ἀλλοτρίου here as masculine and another name for the devil (see note 17); see *Acts of John* 66.3. But it could also be taken as neuter and thus as a reference to "foreign things" (see Luke 16:12).

[27] An unusual metaphorical use of almsgiving.

The Fourth Act of the Holy Apostle Philip
In Azotus, When He Cured Charitine, the Daughter of Nikokleides

1. Now when news circulated widely about the apostle Philip in Azotus because of the wonders he was performing, many ran to meet him and from that hour they were healed from their diseases. Also many demons as they were being driven out of people were crying out like they were being whipped and they were saying: "Have you come here, Philip, to drive us from this place? Look, we admit to being defeated by the name of Jesus." Then as the crowds were staring, they were saying: "Truly he is a man of God." Others were saying: "Why not presume that he is a magician?" Some of the leading citizens and wise men were ridiculing his words, though they were astonished at the healings. The wives of some leading citizens were saying: "Truly a holy spirit is in him"; and they were saying: "Blessed be his God." They were receiving his words like honey. But others were reviling him, saying that he separates husbands and wives, for he teaches that purity sees God and says that childbearing is a sorrow.

2. Then Philip turned aside and said to himself: "O Lord Jesus, sweet voice of the Father, you appeared to the world as a foreigner and made us like foreigners, in order that we might become worthy of your confidence. Where can I lay my head, as you have said? or Who will receive me as a guest in this city?" As he was thinking these things, suddenly a beautiful child appeared to Philip on his right side, pointing out to him a shelter among some storehouses in which many foreigners were lodging. So Philip went in as a foreigner. Now the storehouses belonged to a certain great archivist named Nikokleides, a friend of the king. He had a beloved daughter named Charitine. And his palace was in the midst of the storehouses.

3. Now Philip sat praying by himself during the night, and after this he was speaking aloud: "O my soul, do you seek to eat food? Blessed be God that you do not have bread to eat nor water to drink until the week is complete, until I perceive the heart of the people in this city. O my soul, how did this mindset come upon you, since you have instead the spiritual food of the Lord? For I have a commitment to see this mission through to the end. I cannot hope in the tangible food of the world. For those who are working in Jesus have everlasting food, for the food of the word is sufficient for them—but it is not possible to be satisfied with this alone until the end because of the disorders of the flesh—so that the man of God might not be separated from the glory of Christ,

which dwells in incomprehensible being and resides in incorruptibility and does not stray. But we have been glorified by a voice so that it might be known that we are not foreigners, but that we are fellow citizens of the heights and relatives of the light. Therefore, do not be troubled, O my soul. Recall the former things and know that bread is not your food. Receive the heavenly food in order that you might draw your friends with yourself into life. Know yourself, who you are. Keep away from drunkenness, so that your kinsmen might be sober. Do not make yourself a stranger. Take the food of the Spirit so that you might not be isolated. Do not fix your eyes on the one who invites you to the pleasure of life, but rather rejoice in the one who leads you up to the heights, and let your friends be extremely joyful. Recall the former way of freedom so that your friends may not go astray. Make yourself miserable. Do not long for meals[28] as a way that you might receive strength. Acknowledge Christ, the Son of the living God. Wear your garment[29] wisely, knowing that your struggle is not insignificant. For you will receive imperishable things in radiant eternity. But go, do not be distressed—because the enemy has mastered you in these ways—for already you are near to being rescued. In this marketplace there are some who buy and sell in the excitement of deception, but for us Jesus Christ is the honest merchant. Let us not be troubled by hardship, for we will be undisturbed in rest. These things I declare to you, O my soul."

4. While Philip, the servant of Christ, was saying these things, Charitine, the daughter of Nikokleides who had a severe disfigurement in her right eye, was weeping as she listened to the apostle through the entire night. When morning came, she went in to her father and said: "My lord and my sweetest father, look straight at me and pay close attention to the disfigurement of my eye, how I am being mocked.[30] Because my girlfriends laugh at me and I am ashamed; I cannot bear the pain." Her father said to her: "O my beloved soul, what other physician might I bring in to you? Have I not brought in Leucius, the physician of the king, and the physicians of the entire palace, and even Eleides, the queen's

---

[28] The unusual term τὰ μίσσα is a relatively late Greek term, influenced by Latin, meaning "what is brought to the table."

[29] "Garment" (ἔνδυμα) here is used as a metaphor for the body; but garment as a particular type of clothing is also important in the *Acts of Philip* (see 2.1; *Mart.* 29).

[30] The following section (*APh* 4.4, lines 7–43) is missing in *Xenophontos 32*, which resumes only at the start of *APh* 4.5; we translate the remainder of section 4 from *Vaticanus graecus 824* (see note 31).

eunuch, as well as Selgia, the queen's handmaiden, with remedies and every treatment, and no one was able to cure you?" And she said: "I know, father, I know that you have become exhausted on my account. But what I now request, do for me. Listen, during this past night I heard the voice of a certain foreign physician and he was proclaiming in your storehouses about strange remedies. That one alone is able to cure me. For while I was listening to him, I was experiencing great relief from my pains. For this reason I urge you, father, and I beg you, call that one to me; I know that I will be cured."

So he went quickly to the storehouses and was searching for the foreigner. And when he found Philip seated there, he said: "Are you the foreign physician who has taken up residence in this city?" Then Philip replied and said: "Jesus is my physician, the healer of things both hidden and visible. Therefore, I am departing with you." So Philip rose and went into the father's house and found his daughter weeping bitterly.

Her father said: "Why are you weeping, child? Look, I have brought the physician." She said: "Wonderful, father, for today you have refreshed my soul." The apostle said to her: "Do not fear, girl. The remedies of my physician will now grant a cure to you." When the girl heard this, she fell on her face and prostrated herself before him, saying: "I prostrate myself before the physician who is in you. Look, I am about to sprinkle my house with pure water for the entrance of your physician, and when I have taken off my fine linens I will spread them under his feet. Man of the true God, help me, for I know that you can." And she said to her father: "Let us bring him further inside, so that the man of God might see the disfigurement that is all over my face."

When Philip saw it, he was comforting her as well as her father, teaching them and imparting the things about Jesus, that "he alone is the only begotten Son of the God of heaven; if you believe in him, you will live forever and ever."[31]

5. When she went to the apostle, she said: "Please show me your dwelling." Philip replied: "My home is not on earth. But I see in you the appropriately youthful reasoning of knowledge. Therefore Jesus himself will make known to you the dwelling places on high, where there is eternal rest." She said to Philip: "While you speak with me, I do not perceive

---

[31] We resume with *Xenophontos 32* in section 5, which presents a longer text than that found in *Vaticanus graecus 824*.

my pains; but when you are silent, I experience unbearable suffering. Therefore I urge you and I implore the physician in you, heal my suffering and I will be your perfect servant." Philip replied to her: "Rise and spread your right hand over your face as you say 'in the name of Jesus Christ, let the disfigurement of my eye be cured.'" So she did just as he told her, and at that moment she was immediately cured and she was glorifying God.

6. Then her father also believed even as his daughter did, and they were considered worthy of the seal in the Lord. And there was great joy in their house, and many servants and many maidservants as well as children and infants believed in Jesus. Then after Charitine made her appearance and clothing male, she was following Philip in the faith of Christ, glorifying God. To him be the glory forever.

THE FIFTH ACT OF THE HOLY APOSTLE PHILIP
IN THE CITY OF NIKATERA

1. Now when Philip, the apostle of Christ, determined to go up to the city called Nikatera, many disciples followed him, and they were rejoicing exceedingly as they walked along with him and beheld the grace of the revelation of Christ. Philip was among them both day and night and did not cease conversing with them and teaching them about the mighty acts of God, salvation, gentleness, hope, and the sweet smell[32] of faith. He was teaching them that in the fear of God they should receive the instruction of Christ. And the brothers were filled with the Spirit because of all the things being said by him.

2. When Philip went up to the city and those with him, the whole city was stirred up because Philip, the disciple of Christ, had come. And people were disturbed, saying to one another: "What should we do about him? For if we give in to him, the whole city will follow him; it is no small matter if this one should settle here." But Philip was praying to himself and saying: "Lord Jesus Christ, do not abandon us, because we are traveling in your presence and we have every hope in you."

3. The brothers were asking: "Where should we stay?" Philip said: "Take courage and do not be afraid, because he is not abandoning us,

---

[32] We translate the text of the Greek edition here, εὐωδίαν τῆς πίστεως. The manuscript has εὐοδίαν τῆς πίστεως ("straight way of faith"), perhaps explained by the fact that omega and omicron were pronounced the same during the scribe's time. Note that the former expression does occur in the manuscript in paragraph 3.

the one in whom we have hoped with all our heart since we have trusted in him. Therefore he will help us, only let us be steadfast, knowing that Jesus Christ will be our good law. Therefore we proceed in his peace to proclaim the grace of the gospel and the sweet smell of faith and his noble gentleness and the fellowship that exists among the saints, since we also have partaken from his understanding and we have done so forever. He will strengthen us to be participants in his love, which we also have come to know through him, that we might receive power in his grace, which he has shown us, as well as our salvation and living hope forever—even life firmly established—which he made known to us. We have also received zeal and the holy service, for which he deemed us worthy."

4. While Philip was saying these things, the brothers were distressed because they beheld the commotion of the city. And he said to them: "Do not let your mind be terrified, for Christ is with us, the just athlete who is able to deliver us. For he is the one who saves us from every distress, and he will deliver us from every trial, and he will not neglect us in all the tribulations as he fights on our behalf. He also saves us from every trick and deception of the devil, whom the Lord Jesus will rebuke at the end." When Philip had said these things, the brothers took courage and were filled with joy—indeed their hearts were filled with joy—because he was encouraging and comforting them in the grace of Christ.

5. Now it happened after these words that the crowds of the city ran up, since they were provoked to anger against Philip. And these and their leaders were saying: "What should we do to him? For we have heard that he has done signs and wonders in other cities, and no one was able to harm him. But his teaching is that husbands and wives should separate, since he declares that purity, as he puts it, associates with God, and he teaches belief in the name of a certain Jesus. Now then, since he has not yet found a residence in our city, let us expel him before he subverts our wives and they are deceived by him."

6. Now there were also Jews speaking many harsh words against Philip, because he was destroying their traditions. And a certain one of their leaders by the name of Ireos answered and said to them: "Listen to me, friends and fellow citizens, let us not rise up against a stranger with wrongdoing and violence. Rather, let us hear and examine his teaching, and then let us dare to do what we must." Now Ireos was a rich man among them, wishing gently to thwart their intention; for he was also intelligent and good and a hater of wrongdoing. So no one dared oppose him, except that the people were irritated with him because he did not

speak evil with them against Philip, nor did he join in with their disturbance. And they were saying to one another that perhaps Ireos believed in Philip and was bringing him into his house. "Come, let us startle him by rising up against him." And again they were saying: "The stranger would not enter into Ireos' house unless Ireos has parted with some of his wealth, because this impostor hates the rich. And so he will follow the stranger, for he fights hard on his behalf."

7. After Ireos withdrew from their gathering, he went to Philip and greeted him first. And Philip said to him: "You are favored in the peace of Christ, because there is no deceit in your soul." And Ireos said: "I will follow you, but what then will become of me?" And Philip said: "You have resolved wholly in your heart to seek real life. I tell you, you yourself will be saved and your household and all those with you. And just as you fought on my behalf in the crowd, the Lord Jesus will grant you rest in the day of judgment." 8. Ireos said: "Be assured, man of God, that I have come to meet you without deceit. Therefore do not ignore me, because I have prepared my soul for salvation." Philip said to him: "The Lord will fulfill your longing. Only do not hesitate with regard to preparation, on account of which you have come to us." He said to Philip: "I am not turning back while I have hope." Philip said: "Permit no wrongdoing, and part with your wife." When Ireos heard this, he rushed off, and Philip marveled. Ireos was saying to himself in his heart: "May it be granted to me, Lord, to fight even until death on behalf of your apostle."

9. When he entered into his house, his wife Nerkella said to him: "I heard concerning you that you thwarted the plan of the Jews with regard to a certain foreign magician, Philip." He said: "Would that we were worthy that our house might be a dwelling place for his God." She said to him: "I do not want him to enter into my house, because he separates husbands and wives. I will go away to my parents' house and I will not leave my dowry behind in your house. I will also take away my servants whom I brought to you, some four hundred bodies. Twenty years I have lived together with you and I have not opposed you with few or many words. Moreover, what will you do about your children, if you bring that magician here? For surely there will be confusion in your house." 10. Ireos said to her with gentleness: "Indeed I believe that even you yourself will believe in the God being preached by the foreigner, because he is better for us than our futile wealth." His wife said to him: "Rise, eat, drink, and be glad, for you cannot deceive me." He said to her: "How is it right for me to eat and drink while the man of God is hungry in our city?

If you see him, you will believe that he is holy. Therefore repress your hysteria and your disbelief, in order that I might relate to you something of the knowledge that is in him. Know, therefore, that he is a man of God, that there is grace in his face." 11. His wife said to him: "Is his God like the gods of our city, made of gold and secured in a temple?" He said: "Nothing like that, for his God is the God who lives in the heavens, able to shatter the arrogant, to do away with the evildoers. But the gods of our city are an exercise of craftsmanship by the impious." His wife said to him: "Whether it is the will of the God of whom you speak or your own desire, I will not oppose you."

12. [". . .][33] rise, enter into my house, and rest yourself in peace." Then Philip quickly reported to him everything that had happened in his house and all the ways in which his wife rebelled against him. And Ireos was astonished at how he knew everything. And Philip said: "Know, child, that even if I am one of the least and humble, I also have a contest approaching in order that I might complete this mission that was entrusted to me. If you wish, I will even tell you all the words that were spoken in your house." But Ireos begged him not to speak of the proof against his wife.

13. Those who were with Philip said to him: "Blessed one, how long will we be prisoners in this place? Since the Lord Jesus has prepared this man, let us depart with him in peace." And Ireos was overjoyed because he heard this from Philip's disciples. And he bowed down and was prostrating himself, inviting them to go with him. Philip was moved by compassion for him, saying: "Stand up." For Jesus had appeared to Philip, saying: "Raise him up and proceed with him, for his house is worthy of my peace." When Philip had raised up and embraced Ireos, he said: "Let us depart as you wish." Philip's disciples rejoiced, and Ireos was walking before them.

14. When the city leaders and the entire multitude saw Ireos hastening along in this way, leading Philip and those with him with honor, they were all troubled as well as the whole city. They said: "Look how the magician follows Ireos. But let us not yield to them." When Ireos reached the gateway of his house, he called out for them to open the gates: "Open for the man of God." The doorkeeper quickly opened them,

---

[33] The abrupt beginning of paragraph 12 suggests that the scribe has omitted something. It seems that we must presuppose that Ireos has left his wife and joined Philip, which is the scenario we find in *Vaticanus graecus 824*.

and when Philip went in along with his disciples, he said: "Peace has come to this house today." Ireos ran in to where his wife was, covered by seven layers, and said to her: "Get up and see our joy which has entered into our house today. Take off these garments of yours interwoven with gold and put on others that will adorn you for immortality." She said: "Keep away from me. Since not even those from the household have seen my face, how is it possible that I shall let myself be seen by a stranger?"

15. Because he[34] wished to go out, Ireos ordered his servants to carry the chairs of gold and place them before the gateway so Philip might sit as well as those with him. But when Philip saw this, he said to the servants: "Take them away, for we will not sit upon them." Ireos said: "Do not grieve me." Philip replied: "I do not grieve anyone, rather I give rest to all. But as to gold and silver there is no need at all, for these things are worthless because they will be destroyed by fire. What advantage is there for a man to adorn himself with gold when his soul is going to be afflicted by fire? Or, what advantage is the bloom of youth, since beauty fades away? Wealth in this world will not persist." 16. Ireos said: "Then will I live, for I have pain in my heart over my past sin?" Philip said: "Do not be afraid, nor be doubtful. For Jesus is able to erase your sins which you committed in ignorance. But what about your wife who said to you while wearing garments interwoven with gold and covered by seven layers: 'Keep away from me, because I will not come out into the presence of a stranger'?"

17. When the doorkeeper heard this she immediately believed in Christ, because the words said by the lady of the house were known in this way to Philip. Moreover, the maidservant said to herself: "Would then that I knew for certain what repentance is, truly I would believe." When Philip perceived her thoughts he said to her: "I say to you, woman, you shall be saved." And she rejoiced over the word that he spoke to her; and her name was Marklaina.

18. Meanwhile Ireos again went in to his wife and said: "How long will such forgetfulness about yourself last? Get up! Look! He is truly a man of God, for the words which we spoke between ourselves and all that happened in private he reported to me." His wife said to him: "And is this a great thing, that he reported my words to you? Go! Do not deceive me! As for your own affairs, do what you want."

---

[34] Although the verb has no explicit subject, the logic of the paragraph indicates that it is Philip; the French translation assumes it is Ireos' wife.

19. Philip realized that Ireos was upset by his wife, and he began to speak to Jesus: "Lord Jesus Christ, Son of God, firstborn of all creation, I beg you, show me what I should do, because you have indicated to me that this house is worthy of your service. Accordingly reveal to me now about Ireos' wife Nerkella, whether she is worthy of your grace." As Philip was saying this the Savior appeared to him and said: "Do not be afraid nor hesitate to carry out my teaching. Such is the word which I told you: both will be saved." When Philip heard this, he was astonished by Nerkella's stubbornness, and once more rejoiced with even greater joy because of Ireos, that he might be done with his confusion.

20. Now it happened that after these words all the unbelief of Ireos' wife fell away, and she said to her husband: "Blessed is the one who is not undecided." Ireos said to her: "What happened to you? or What did you gaze upon? or From where did you get this saying? Now if you have put away your error, the God of this man has the power to do away with all your passions. So get up and come to him. Do not look upon wealth that perishes, or on your beauty." And what did his wife say? "What should we do about our sons or daughters or servants and about our possessions, if the foreigner literally said: 'Unless you abandon your wealth, you cannot be saved'? Further, what should we do since we have promised our two sons in marriage according to our social status? And if we become disciples of the foreigner, what will happen?"

21. As she was saying this, her daughter Artemilla heard it and said: "Mother, why are you saying these things? For if there is a certain life into which you and my father will enter, clearly I too wish to share in it." Now Artemilla was exceedingly beautiful. Her mother said to her in gentleness: "Get up, daughter, and take off this garment shot through with gold that you are wearing." And she said: "The will of the foreigner, the man of God, will prevail in everything." Ireos again said to his wife: "Let us go out to him. For if you see him, our entire household will believe in him." And immediately she got up and removed her garments interwoven with gold and put on humble clothing, both she and her daughter. And they went out of the bedroom.

22. Ireos was going before them rejoicing; and their attire was decent and no part of their bodies was uncovered, except perhaps for their eyes. And Ireos said: "Come on, do not hesitate." Then as they came toward Philip and saw him as some great light and the disciples in a circle around him, they were unable to approach him. And Ireos was afraid of Philip over how he had transformed himself in this way. And

they fell on their faces and were weeping, saying: "Be merciful to us." And the whole household was shaken on account of the fear that had fallen upon them.

23. Now when Philip realized that they were not able to bear the intensity of the light, he remembered Jesus, and he returned to his former appearance. And Philip said: "Get up and do not be afraid." And they got up and Nerkella said to Philip: "I will be blessed if I am found worthy to have you stay in my house. For woe, woe is me over my unbelief. Therefore, do not consider the thoughts that came into my heart and my words about you in private, because I did not realize who you were." And Ireos was rejoicing over her words. And his daughter, when she saw her mother weeping, her tears also flowed upon her cheeks. Likewise the men and maidservants were shaken at such a sight.

24. Then Philip said: "You will all be saved by Jesus." And he addressed Nerkella: "If you wish to live, despise everything about your present life and your beauty." She replied and said: "Whatever you command I will do so that salvation might be mine." In the same way her daughter said: "I beseech you, man of God, I too wish to be saved." And Philip said: "Insofar as you also abandon the beauty of your body, you will be saved." She said: "Certainly, choose me also to be among those being saved and reckon me with them. For I have already despised everything about this worthless life."

25. When Philip heard this he began to teach:[35] "Blessed are those who are straightforward in the word of Jesus, because these will inherit the earth. Blessed are those who have chosen to hate the glory of this world, because these will be glorified. Blessed are those who have accepted the word of God, because these will inherit imperishability." After Philip said this, all were filled with joy, and they said to Philip: "Blessed are we because we have been considered worthy of your words."

26. And Ireos was glad because Philip entered into his house. And he brought him bread and vegetables, and he begged that Philip might partake as well as those with him. But Philip said: "I am not eating until I complete my contest, which has been ordained beforehand for me in this city." Then he ordered his disciples to take the bread and vegetables and he prayed. And after he broke the bread he gave it to them to eat.

---

[35] The beatitudes are absent from *Vaticanus graecus 824*, perhaps owing to their excessive asceticism.

They said to him: "You too should eat with us so that you might be able to withstand what is going to happen to you." He said to them: "As far as I am concerned, what God wills, this will come about."

27. After Philip's disciples departed, a large crowd assembled in Ireos' house. And they were listening to his word and believing, exalting in the glory of Jesus, while those who were sick were being healed and the unclean spirits were fleeing. And all were saying: "Blessed be the God of Philip, because in his own tenderness he has been merciful to us. To him be the glory forever, amen."

THE SIXTH ACT OF PHILIP THE APOSTLE IN THE CITY OF NIKATERA

1. Now while Philip was in the house of Ireos and all the brothers and sisters were gathered together, all the Jews and the pagans in the city were stirred up. And they spoke against Ireos and Philip because Philip was in the house of Ireos, and they said: "It is no small concern and distress to us, because the magician called Philip is deceiving many." And there was much strife, because Ireos had believed in Christ with his entire household. And they were saying: "If we had known sooner and had completely driven out the magician, or even shut the city gates, the sorcerer would not have entered. But let us send some men to Ireos of his social rank who will remove him from the stranger's deception, or let us bring him to the city hall."

2. When they had summoned seven elite men, they requested them to go, saying: "Say to Ireos, 'the entire city is waiting on you.'" So after they departed, they stood before the gateway; and no one among them dared to issue a summons on account of the multitude of disciples. When a certain maidservant went out and saw them, she said: "You unjust men, why do you stand before our gates?" For she had heard personally about their irritation, and for this reason she called them unjust. And when she had run in and shut the doors with haste, she went to Ireos and said: "Master, seven men are standing before the gateway and their faces are full of wickedness and evil." So Ireos rose and went out, and when he observed them he smiled. Then they said to him: "Hail, foremost and great one of our city." And Ireos said: "Why have you come? Or do you believe you can remove me from the righteous man? Why are you standing like this in wickedness?" And those delegated[36] said: "Virtually the

---

[36] The word here is ἄρχοντες, lit. "rulers," "leaders," "officials."

entire city sent us, and we have stood for three hours before your gateway. So if you are willing, come along." So Ireos followed them, smiling and concerned about nothing.

3. Now when the authorities saw him, they stood up and they were shocked, because he was not dressed like the day before or earlier, and because he was not in the midst of a crowd of slaves, rather only twelve slaves were following him. And they said to one another: "What should we say, because he is our superior, and yet only twelve follow him? How has the foreigner cast a spell on him? But if it is proper, let us ask him and he may tell us what he was taught by him." Now a certain one of them, Onesimos, going first said to Ireos: "I know that I am not able by rank to speak with you, but I appeal to you to tell us what novel thing you heard when you were deceived by the foreigner. Now then deliver him to us in order that you might be saved as well as your household, because the entire city has risen in rebellion against you. Therefore, get a hold of yourself and act like a leader in the city, since you are so powerful. Now why also are you behaving as though in a trance? Who deceived you in this manner if not that magician? We do not wish to be deceived in this way by you, because his entire teaching is about separating husbands and wives and preaching purity; and he strongly affirms, as he calls it, the resurrection of the dead. So do not keep silent with us, but answer us even one word, because we, the authorities and the entire city, have assembled on your account."

4. Ireos replied: "Why should I today be examined by you on account of the righteous man? Keep away from him and cease your disturbance, lest the man of God be angered and call upon his own God and burn all of you up with fire."

5. But the authorities and the crowds shouted out: "You cannot persuade us to ignore the foreigner in the city. For we do not hold fast to his teaching, since we have our own gods." Then the Jews shouted out more loudly: "Remove this evil and foreign teaching from our city."

Now when Ireos saw that he was unable to turn back the crowds, he withdrew to his house as did the slaves who were with him. And when Philip looked him in the face, he said to Ireos: "You have not been frightened by anything, have you?" And Ireos said: "I will not turn back, even if I would have to die. Yet listen, blessed one, because the entire city has risen up against us. If then you know that you can somehow contend against them, tell me. But if not, I will write to the governor. For he has the power to rescue you. But the crowd is undisciplined and perhaps they may kill you." The apostle said: "You all should not be afraid, for Jesus in whom I have hoped has the power to contend on my behalf and rescue me." And he did not wish to partake of food "unless first," he said: "I compete in my contest and prevail in the glory of my Christ, and then I will break my fast, rejoicing exceedingly in the name of Jesus."

6. And while Philip was in Ireos' house, the entire city and the authorities ran together to it and shouted out: "Give us the deceiver, give us the magician, bring out the magician!" Now when Philip perceived that they were about to throw the house into disorder on account of him, he opened the gate and went out together with those with him; Ireos also went out with them. And the entire crowd shouted out: "Look, this is the magician." Then Ireos ordered three hundred slaves to accompany Philip. And when the crowds had seized him, they brought him into the council chamber in order that they might whip him. Now Philip's disciples were weeping. But the apostle silenced them and censured them, saying: "By faith and perseverance we will conquer the opponent." And the crowds shouted out: "Tightly bind the hands and feet of the deceiver, and thus whip him."

7. When Ireos observed their anger, he ran up the steps of the council chamber and cried out in a loud voice: "You cannot strike this man without cause, for even Caesar hears about such things." But when the crowds saw Ireos standing there, they were enraged and said: "Let us not listen to Ireos, but let us do what we are daring to do." And they approached Philip in order to whip him. But when Ireos came down he dragged Philip from them, seizing him by the hand, and Ireos said: "Who among you is powerful enough to come up against this righteous man?" But Philip replied with gentleness: "What evil did I do and what injustice did I bring about in your city that you intend to whip me?" And Ireos said: "Look, you all say that this one is a magician. Prove it!" Then they cried out: "He has brought a new and strange teaching to our city. 'Remain pure,' he says, 'and you will live and you will be stars in heaven.' And he speaks about a crucified god, who is son of a living God."

8. When Philip heard this, he said: "I know that should I wish it, you could not whip me. For I will call him in gentleness and he will strike you with blindness. But I will not boast in noble birth and wealth." Now they knew that Philip was of noble birth and that he left behind much wealth and in this way followed Jesus. Then they were afraid of him, because he said he would strike them with blindness.

9. Now a murmuring arose among the Jews about Philip's words and they wished out of rivalry to debate with him. Then a certain one of them named Aristarchos, an only son who was prominent among the Jews, said to Philip in front of all of them: "Debate with me about Jesus, the crucified one. For you say he is God, and that in his name you do wonders, which we have seen. So do not be eager to blind us, for I know that you are capable of it. Rather, accept my words, and do not resolve to deceive us by your magic. For I myself am great among the Jews and should I allow it, they will stone you and those with you."

10. And he seized Philip's beard in order to drag him. Yet Philip felt no pain, but being mildly angered by those present, he said: "Look, I tell you that this hand will be withered, and your ears painfully deaf, and your right eye maimed because you threatened to stone me and provoked me with my beard."

11. Now this sudden and wondrous event was a sight to behold. Philip said: "I beseech you, Christ, do not delay." And immediately his eye was made hollow as though it were not there, and his ears were in no little pain, and his right hand hung withered, and he cried out: "Have mercy on me, Philip, for I already admitted that you can do whatever you wish." Then he urged the Jews who were with him that they might appeal to Philip so that being moved by compassion he might cure him. So all raised their voice, saying: "Truly you have a god with you, stranger. Heal the leader of our people, for truly as human beings we cannot fight with God."

12. Philip turned to Ireos and said: "Approach and place your right hand upon his head and make the sign of the cross of Christ, and he will be cured." So when Ireos approached him, he said: "In the name of the crucified one, be whole again." And immediately he was greatly alarmed and was looking around at the crowds. And because he was looking around for some time, Philip said to him: "What are you observing in this way?" And he said: "I saw a child coming from heaven to you, who spoke to you so that you might heal me. And now I am looking around to see where he is. And just now I see him again, rising up quickly into heaven." Philip said: "The handsome child whom you saw, this is Jesus, who never abandons us. So you too, believe in him, so that you might live forever." Then Aristarchos said to Philip: "I know that you can become angry, but I adjure you by the crucified one, do not again in your rage inflict pain upon me. As I asked you before, have a discussion with me, because I wish to debate carefully about the Messiah." And

the crowds said: "We ask you, Philip, do not become angry if you are refuted, nor too fearful for your teaching. For when we have listened to both of your arguments, we will be the judges of the truth. And if you prevail, we will all believe in the Messiah being proclaimed by you."

13. Philip smiled and said to Aristarchos: "If you wish, speak first." When Aristarchos turned his eyes to the Jews who were with him, he said: "Stand with me and let us together resist this foreigner, so that after taking up residence in our city he might not turn everyone to his side." And they said: "We are not in the same boat as you who have claimed that you will not be struck again. But if you as the leader of the synagogue are capable, speak. For have you perhaps forgotten how he struck you with terrible pains?" Then Aristarchos said to Philip: "Do you accept the prophetic utterances?" Philip said: "Because of your unbelief you had need of prophets." The Jew said: "Are you ignorant, Philip, that it is written: 'Who will explain your mighty acts, O God?' and 'No one can ever know your glory' and that 'Your glory has filled the earth' and that 'The Lord is the judge of the living and the dead' and that 'God is a consuming fire and he will burn up his enemies' and that 'One God made everything'? Then how can you yourself say, Philip, that Mary gave birth to Jesus in an incorruptible way, and that he is God? And how can you say that he was crucified, and how can you fight on his behalf? But doubtless you will thoroughly refute me saying that this one is the power of God and the wisdom of God, who was present with God when God made the world. For this I do not deny, since the first scripture says: 'Let us make a human being according to our image and likeness.' For if I am silent about these things, you will refute me."

14. But Philip smiled and in exaltation said to the whole crowd: "Listen to me, and be judges of the truth. For the prophet Isaiah says concerning the Messiah: 'Behold my servant whom I have chosen, in whom I am well pleased. I will put my Spirit upon him.' And concerning his cross he has said: 'Like a sheep he was led to slaughter, and like a lamb he remained silent before the one who sheared him. But concerning his generation, who will tell of it?' And again: 'My back I gave to lashes, and my cheeks to slaps, and I did not turn away my face from the shame of being spit upon.' And at another place: 'I held out my hands to a disobedient and rebellious people, and I revealed myself to those who did not seek me, and was found by those who did not ask for me.' And David says concerning him: 'You are my son, today I have begotten you. Ask of me and I will give you the nations as your inheritance.' And

concerning his resurrection and concerning Judas, he says: 'Lord, why have those who oppress me multiplied? Many have turned against me, many are saying to my soul: There is no salvation for him in his God.' And he continues with the rest of the psalm. You see all the prophecies have cried out concerning him. Once more David: 'I have seen my Lord before me forever,' and so forth. But David died and we are acquainted with his tomb. So all these things have been said about the Messiah and his resurrection from the dead. Take also from the Twelve Prophets: 'Say to the daughter of Zion: "Look, your king is coming mounted on a young colt."' And another: 'Out of Egypt I have called my son.' The whole chorus of the prophets and all the patriarchs have proclaimed concerning the coming of Christ."[37]

15. Aristarchos replied, saying: "Philip, this one is called Jesus and Messiah. Indeed I know that Isaiah has spoken with reference to an anointed one: 'These things the Lord said to my anointed Lord †I did not hold back his right hand to listen before†[38] the nations will hope.'" But the Jews were quarreling with Aristarchos because they said: "You yourself have called to mind all the more the things that have been written concerning the Messiah." And the entire crowd was saying: "Why are we striving jealously against Philip with respect to these matters?" And the city authorities were saying: "Surely our gods brought Philip into the city in order that we might learn that they are deaf and blind and worthless. And he himself has guided us to the genuine truth. Therefore what charge might we find against him? On the contrary even the Jew who debated with him has shown all the more the hidden glory in the prophets concerning the Messiah. For this reason, since we have examined the words of both speakers and have seen that Christ[39] has been revealed beyond a doubt by everything, let us appeal to Philip so that he might dwell in our city always for our salvation." Now Ireos was extremely joyful of heart over the words of Philip, and Philip would not cease glorifying God.

16. Now as the city authorities were evaluating the words of the apostle and the Jews, suddenly a stretcher was brought in upon which was lying a dead man who was his father and mother's only son, who

---

[37] Χριστός is used throughout these sections, but at this point we translate "Christ" instead of Messiah to capture the theological transition of the narrative.

[38] The text is corrupt here; see the Greek edition, pp. 206-7 n. 12.

[39] Again one detects a transition from Messiah to Christ.

was exceedingly rich. Now there were twelve slaves carrying the stretcher with the dead man, who were going to be burned together with the corpse. When the city authorities and all the crowd observed that the man was truly dead, they cried out: "Here is a truly great contest for the Christian. For if a god is in him, doubtless he will also raise him, and we will believe in him and we ourselves will burn the idol temples that are here."

17. As they were discussing these things in this way, the parents were weeping. Then Philip was moved with compassion and said to the father of the boy and his mother: "What will you do if I raise your son?" They replied to him: "We will do whatever you wish." Now the slaves who were going to be burned together with the boy were gesturing to the apostle to keep them in mind. So Philip also said: "You will give these slaves to me." The parents said: "We will give you three hundred others as well as these. We will also give you silver and gold and garments interwoven with gold and much wealth. We will even give you the twelve gods of solid gold, after we have broken them in pieces, for charity. And what's more we will believe that the only living God is the God of Philip, the one who raises the dead." And they confirmed their words in the presence of the prefect.

18. When Philip stared out, he saw Jesus standing on his right and saying to him: "Do not be afraid, because through me the dead one will be raised." Now his name was Theophilos. So Philip ordered the crowd to stand back from the stretcher, for they were crushing one another. Philip said to Aristarchos the Jew: "Come now, Jew, look, a corpse is lying here. So, if you can do anything, raise him." Since he was being pressured by all, Aristarchos reluctantly approached the dead man, touched his face, spit upon him a great deal, and dragged him by the hand. But the dead man lay there like a stone. And when he could do nothing, the crowds cried out: "Remove the Jew from our midst." And he withdrew, ashamed. And Ireos said: "Citizens and you who continually oppose God, you have dared to blaspheme, saying: 'Philip is a magician.' If the God in him was not good, you all would have been put to death."

19. Nereus the father of the one who had died said: "Let my only son be raised, and I will contend against the Jews." Philip said to the father of the boy: "Unless you promise not to do harm to the Jews, your son will not be raised." The father of the boy said: "I will do your bidding, only raise my son." Now all the crowds and the authorities wondered as they were considering what Philip would do, whether he would be able to raise the dead man.

20. Then with no further delay Philip, after looking up to heaven, said a prayer. And when he approached the stretcher, he laid his hands upon the boy, saying: "O God and father of our Lord Jesus Christ, you who always listen to me. Open the heavens and let my secret petition enter, and grant life to your servant Theophilos." Then breath went into the boy and he opened his eyes and was watching Philip. And when the crowds saw what had happened, they were pressing upon one another to approach the stretcher since they wished to see the miracle. But Philip proceeded to pray a second time, and said to the boy: "In the name of Jesus Christ: speak, rise, and walk!" And at once Theophilos cried out: "There is one God, the God of Philip, Christ Jesus, who has given me life." And immediately he stood up. And when the crowds saw the boy standing, they called out as with one voice: "There is one God, the God of Philip, Christ Jesus, who raises the dead." And they were debating with one another and saying: "What greater miracle do we still have to see? We ourselves confess on the basis of this happening that there is no other God living except Philip's God, who is doing these mighty deeds through him."

21. So from his miracle three thousand souls believed in Christ. And the father of the boy and his mother glorified God exceedingly. And all the slaves whom they had promised to set free he ordered to come to the place where the boy had been raised. And when Philip fixed his eyes on the slaves, he said to them: "Slaves until today but now free people through Christ, do not neglect your own salvation." And the slaves answered: "We too will practice piety through you." Then before everyone the prefect crowned them to signify their freedom. And the father and mother of the boy rejoiced exceedingly over them, and because they had seen their son fully raised. Then the father said to Ireos: "What are we going to do about the Jews who are rising up against Philip?" Ireos said: "Philip is a good man and he does not allow us to respond in kind."

22. Then the disciples prepared bread and vegetables, because Philip had said: "After my victory I will break my fast, rejoicing exceedingly in my Christ." When Philip entered in, he partook of the food with gusto. And for five days he was giving thanks to God for the souls that had been saved. And all together were saying to God: "Amen." May the peace of Christ be with us forever, amen.

The Seventh Act of the Holy Apostle Philip
In the City of Nikatera, Where Nerkella Believed

1. Now Nerkella, the wife of Ireos, and her daughter Artemilla rejoiced because of Philip, along with the doorkeeper, and they believed in the Lord. Then the apostle blessed all those who had believed and said: "Amen, peace be upon you." Then Nerkella and her daughter Artemilla appealed to him that he might also bless them. Philip said: "See! The Savior is producing this request in you, and blessing is in your souls."

2. Ireos said to Philip: "Where do you wish us to build a gathering place[40] in the name of Christ?" Philip said: "Build from your own resources and not from ill-gotten gains." Nereus, the father of the boy who had been raised, said: "May you rather consider me worthy to build it." And there was great joy, and the house was not able to contain the crowds entering in. When Ireos and Nereus the father of the raised boy went out of the house, they conferred with one another about the structure and said: "Let us cast lots as to the place in which we should build, whether on your land or on mine, most excellent Nereus. If you wish the structure to be on your land, I will not cause you distress. Only let God's will be done." And when they had negotiated the manner in which it was necessary to build, the two of them spent much gold. And the multitude of the brothers and sisters was rejoicing at the speed of the construction.

3. The Jews alone were jealous and they were saying to one another: "We have no pretext for hindering them because of Philip's miracles. Rather, let us keep away from the foreigner, lest we suffer some wrong such as befell Aristarchos. Indeed, let us keep away from them, for their grace and power and glory is truly from God."

4. Now after these words Philip entered into the building and was extremely glad; and he was speaking boldly in Christ. And all those who believed came into the gathering place and were marveling and rejoicing at Philip's teaching, and there was great reverence among them. For Philip was teaching them and calling to mind the mighty deeds of Christ, so that their understanding might be rightly guided by insight. And the gift of God was remaining in him. And his face was cheerful, for there was great wisdom in him on account of good intelligence and divine knowledge, and on account of the kindness of righteousness and on account of steadfastness and on account of the power that he received

---

[40] The building is designated as a συναγωγή, not an ἐκκλησία, though the latter term is used for a building at 11.8.

from Christ, because he gave him a holy glory and the word that had been given to him from God.

5. Now Nerkella, the wife of Ireos, and her daughter Artemilla were extremely glad and relaxed, since Philip had blessed them. He said: "Brothers and sisters, I am giving you commandments so that you will be in the will of Christ. Live in community with one another in purity and do not forget my words, but let them dwell in your hearts; for this is God's will. Do not let arrogance take root in yourselves. Remain in the plantation of Christ so that your blessing may accompany me to the place to which I am departing to preach the grace of Christ."

6. When the brothers and sisters heard this, they moaned and wept exceedingly because he said to them: "I am leaving"; for they did not want him to depart from them. Philip said to them: "Do not be distressed in your hearts, for just as my Lord ordained that I should come to you, so also I am leaving for other cities so that I might accomplish the will of Christ. May the Lord be with you."

7. After Philip said this he prayed with them, said goodbye to everyone, and went out from them, and his disciples with him, as well as all the crowd to load the camels with bread and many supplies for traveling. And for some twenty stadia[41] they were following him. Philip said to them: "Why are you troubling yourselves?" They replied: "So that we may see the ship on which you are embarking." He said: "It is far off." Then he took only five loaves, and after invoking the name of Jesus, he commanded them to turn back to the city with the camels and their plentiful provisions. And he said: "Go in peace."

8. And a voice came from heaven: "Hurry, Philip! I, Jesus, am waiting for you on the ship in the upper harbor,[42] for I will not leave you behind." The brothers and sisters were amazed and believed all the more, and they begged Philip that he might bless them a second time. Philip said to them: "The grace, glory, and love of the Lord Jesus as well as his mercy and blessing will be with you. And let the help of the Lord also accompany you." And everyone said: "Amen!" And again a voice was heard: "Yes indeed, amen, amen, amen!" Both now and always and forever and ever, amen.

---

[41] About two and a half miles.

[42] Is this a geographical feature as suggested in the translation above, or is it intended as a metaphor for the journey to the upper harbor of heaven as the French translation takes it with reference to *Acts of Philip* 3.8 (see Greek edition, p. 232 n. 10)?

74   The *Acts of Philip*

THE EIGHTH ACT OF THE HOLY APOSTLE PHILIP
WHERE THE KID OF THE GOAT AND THE LEOPARD BELIEVE
IN THE WILDERNESS[43]

Atheniensis 346 (G)

1. When the Savior divided the apostles according to city and region so that each one of them might proceed to the place that had been appointed to them by lot, just as they were assigned, the lot came first to Peter to depart for Rome; and Thomas was committed to depart for all the region of Parthia and India; and it was allotted to Matthew to depart for the interior parts of Pontus; and it was allotted to Bartholomew to depart for Lycaonia; Simon the Cananaean departed for Spain; Andrew for Achaia; John for Asia; and Philip departed for the land of the Greeks. For this is the disposition arranged by the Savior.

2. But when Philip heard the name of the region and the city that had been allotted to him, it seemed harsh to him, and grumbling he wept. Now when he wept, the Savior turned to him with John and Mariamne, his sister (for she was the one who held the register of the regions, and it was she who prepared the bread and the salt, and the breaking of the bread. Martha was the one who served the crowds and worked very much). Mariamne spoke with the Savior about Philip, since he was distressed because of the city to which he was being sent. And she was saying: "My Lord Jesus Christ, it is not pleasing for my brother Philip."

3. And the Savior said to her: "I know that you are good and manly in soul and blessed among women; and the woman's way of thinking has entered into Philip, but the masculine and manly way of thinking is in you. So go with him to every place he goes and keep encouraging him with love and much compassion. For I see that he is a very reckless man, and if we were to leave him alone he would deliver much retribution to each place he passes by. But look, Bartholomew is departing with him and is going to suffer with him in the persecutions and the outrages that will be brought upon him by the people of that place. Again, in like

---

[43] The title for Act 8 found in *Xenophontos 32* (A) agrees on the whole with that of *Vaticanus graecus 824* (V), while *Atheniensis 346* (G) has, "The Act of the Holy Apostle Philip: In Which the Lots of the Holy Apostles Are Assigned." We have translated the title from *Xenophontos*, but since that manuscript breaks off after a few lines in the first paragraph, we switch to *Atheniensis* until it ends in paragraph 15.

manner I am also sending John in order that he might encourage you in the suffering of martyrdom and the redemption of the whole world.

4. "But as for you, Mariamne, change your dress and outward appearance, and put off completely your feminine form and the summer garment with which you have clothed yourself. Do not allow the hem of your garment to drag on the ground, neither tie it up, but trim it with scissors and walk together with your brother Philip to the city called Opheorymos,[44] which means 'Promenade of the Serpents'; for the people of that city worship the mother of the serpents, the Viper. Now when you enter into that city, the serpents of that city must see you dissociated from Eve's appearance, with nothing of a feminine appearance. Since Eve's appearance is woman, she is the form itself; Adam's form is man. And you know that from the beginning hostility arose between Adam and Eve. Such was the beginning of the serpent's standing against that man, and its affection for the woman; and Adam was deceived by his wife Eve. And what the serpent puts off, that is, its poison, he, Adam, put on through Eve; and by this process the ancient enemy found a place in Cain, Eve's son, so that he killed Abel, his brother. So you, Mariamne, flee the poverty of Eve and be rich in yourself.

5. "Look, I am sending you as lambs, I am the shepherd. I am sending you as disciples, I am your teacher. I am sending you as rays, I am your sun. I am sending you as sons, I am your father. I am with you in every place you are going to go. Lift your eyes toward the creation which is in the firmament and gaze at the likeness of the sun, I mean the moon and the stars, the air and the winds. Note how when the sun rises with its light, then it stretches out its rays over all creation. And again when it is about to set, how it takes back and draws its rays to itself before the darkness of night arrives. Similarly the moon does the same thing; it sends its good dew upon the waters and the plants and furnishes life and sweetness to everything. Note how after this the moon changes itself during the winter season; it showers down abundantly in the winter air, until the earth's produce is multiplied and may become food for people and for flocks and for birds of the sky and creeping things and fish which are in the waters, through the providence of my Father and also yours.

6. "For this reason also you, my brothers and sisters, my good plants, the offshoots which have blossomed by my gentleness, do not be

---

[44] The name of the city where the martyrdom takes place varies somewhat in the manuscripts where we find in addition to Opheorymos, Ophiorymos or Ophiorymē.

distressed that I am sending you in this frame of mind; for I am with you in every place you are going to go. For as you proceed along the roads, I will guide you, being your forerunner and preparing your passages for you. On rivers and seas I will be a good shipmaster for you. If you find yourselves in the midst of the waves, I will rise up in order to calm the waves, and I will speak to the wind so that it might blow gently upon you. If you should enter a city and the people of the city should rise up against you and beat you in their synagogues and flog you, I will put medicine on your wounds and on your bruises and I will remove them, and I will be a good doctor for you. And if they brand you with fire, I will put a cool emollient on your burn. If they shed your blood, I will stretch out my shining robe and collect it by an invisible power and send it up to the heights as an offering to my Father in heaven. And your wonders will be glorified on the earth, and they will call your tombs dwelling places of holy bodies, because it has been allotted to you in this way.

7. "Now then, my brothers and sisters, do not fear the bites of the serpents or their poison. For their mouth will be shut before you and their threat will come to naught. If they raise their heads, apply the sign of the Monad to them; if the vipers approach, have the cross ready,[45] and in this way they will bow down their heads."

8. When Philip heard all of these commandments from the Savior and all of these instructions, he wept. And the Savior said to him: "Why are you crying, Philip?" Philip said to him: "I am crying for myself, Lord, because I listened to you readily, and for this reason I am crying, lest I should depart for the lot that was appointed to me, and on account of this they[46] might cause me excessive hardship and bring great persecution and unusual cruelty upon me, since the serpent is their essential nature. Therefore, if that serpent should rise up against me and rage, and thus if it should happen that I am unable to endure him because of his abundant evils, I will repay in kind those who live in that place, and I will have transgressed your commandment that you gave to us not to repay evil with evil, but rather to repay good to those who do us evil. Now then, my Lord, I am crying for myself, because departure to this city is most difficult for me [. . .][47] and the sentence against me will be double if I repay in kind the one who does evil to me."

[45] A way of speaking of the "sign of the cross" (see 6.12; 9.4).
[46] That is, the inhabitants of the region to which Philip is sent.
[47] About four words are illegible here.

9. The Savior answered and said to Philip: "As severe as the sentence is on the one who repays evil for evil, so much greater is the gift that one receives who is capable of doing something evil and does not do it, but rather repays good to the one who does him evil. There is no measure more honorable than such a person, nor greater good than his dignity. Great is this blessing among all the blessings.

10. "You have seen, Philip, all the workmanship of creation that is above and below: light and darkness, water and fire, good and evil; then living beings, indeed I mean people and animals, wild animals and birds and water creatures. You be the judge, Philip, and observe the natural principle working in all the world, and see that whatever does what is good and beautiful is also what multiplies, not what does evil. For light drives away darkness, and light is very glorified. Consider also fire, that it is bad, and water good, and water itself is very plentiful. Indeed, consider too the birds and learn that the dominant among them are few in offspring and in quality, but the meek and tame among them are very numerous. Consider also the animals [. . .],[48] that the predators are few among them [. . .],[49] and such as are good among them are very numerous. The rapacious in the water are few in number compared to the other kinds of creatures in the water.

11. "This is why when the wrath of the judgment upon the Watchers was about to begin in the world, the Lawgiver commanded that Noah should make the ark and bring into the ark all the animals according to their kinds, that he might bring on the deluge and wipe out the evil ones. And he enjoined Noah to bring the birds and the animals into the ark according to their kinds: from those that are clean, seven pairs, male and female; and from those that are unclean, two pairs, male and female—showing by each number the deeds of each. Because he did not forgive them entirely but repaid them in the form of their evildoing; but his forgiveness extended to the seven pairs.

12. "This is also why your brother Peter remembered what had been done by Noah on the day of the punishment of the sinners and said to me: 'Do you wish me to forgive my brother up to seven times, in the same way that Noah forgave?' And I answered him: 'I do not wish you to act according to Noah's model alone, but you are to forgive seventy

---

[48] About four words are illegible here.
[49] About four words are illegible here.

times seven.' Now then, Philip, do not be fainthearted about doing good to those who do evil to you.

13. "Observe also the adversary in the air, in which there are many birds and reptiles, receiving the type for yourself that a person is not defiled by any of them. And what's more many plants grow on the earth from the goodness of my Father in heaven, and dew is supplied to them. His light rises on all the creation, on the evil and the good. Such is also the case with water. For it flows and fills springs and rivers and seas, being the life also of the flavors which are in them, namely, salt waters and those that do not have salt, warm and cold, sweet and bitter. This water exists in the heavens and in all creatures, and it mixes in these according to their differences and according to their own aspects.

14. "You, therefore, become an imitator of all the good things. But pay heed, Philip, also to the illuminators that make the good things and become their imitator. You too, disciples, become imitators of all these things in order that just as they show beneficence by shedding their light on the good and on the evil without discrimination, so too you yourselves should become active for the salvation of the whole world, just as all good disciples and brothers and sisters. And if you are persecuted, endure it; and if you enter into temptation and tribulation which are going to be brought upon you, because of the great tranquility that you possess, taste the future,[50] knowing that you will be shining ones before my Father in heaven and your reward will be very great."

15. Philip was rejoicing and all those with him over the lessons and promises of the Lord. Then Philip went out accompanied by Bartholomew and Mariamne, and after they kissed the right hand of the Savior, they were on their way to the land of the Ophianeans.[51]

Vaticanus graecus 824 (V)

16. Now when they went up into the wilderness of the she-dragons, while they were walking there, suddenly a great leopard came out from the mountain woods. And when he saw the apostles of the Lord, he ran over to them, threw himself at their feet, and spoke to them with a human voice: "I prostrate myself before you, servants of the divine

---

[50] The form γεύσασθε is a conjecture because the reading of the manuscript, γεγέσθαι, does not make sense here.

[51] *Atheniensis 346* (G) ends here; we pick up with *Vaticanus graecus 824* (V), which continues with 16.

greatness and apostles of the only-begotten Son of God. Command me so that I might speak perfectly."

17. Philip said: "In the name of Jesus Christ, speak!" And the leopard assumed a perfect human voice and began to speak: "Listen to me, Philip, you who conduct us to the divine word as one who leads the bride to the bridegroom. It happened in the first part of the night[52] that I passed by a herd of goats opposite the mountain of the she-dragon, the mother of the serpents, and I seized a kid. But when I entered into the woods to eat it, after I struck it, it took on a human voice and cried like a small child, saying to me: 'Leopard, put off your fierce heart and savage intent and put on tameness. For the apostles of the divine greatness are about to pass through this wilderness to fulfill perfectly the promise of the glory of the only-begotten Son of God.' While the kid was admonishing me with these words, I was at a loss with myself, and little by little my heart was changed, and my fierceness was turned into tameness and I refrained from eating it. And as I was listening to its words, I raised my eyes and I saw you passing by, and I knew that you were servants of the good God. So seeing that you were drawing near, I left the kid of the goat alone and came to prostrate myself before you. Now, therefore, I call on you, apostle of Christ, Philip, that you might grant me the right to acquire confidence, and that I might journey together with you to every place you are going, and that I might lay aside my savage nature."

18. The apostle said to the leopard: "Where is the kid?" He replied: "Look! He was thrown under the tree over there." Philip said to Bartholomew: "Let us go so that we might see the one who was struck and then cured, who also healed the one who struck him." So when Philip nodded, the leopard began to lead Philip and those with him, and he brought them to the spot where the kid was lying.

19. Then Philip and Bartholomew said: "Behold we know truly that no one surpasses your compassion, O benevolent Jesus. For you precede us and correct and instruct us through these animals, so that we might believe still more and complete with zeal that which was entrusted to us. Now then, Lord Jesus Christ, come and grant life and breath and a firm constitution to these animals, that they might forsake their savage and beastly nature, and enter into tameness and no longer eat flesh, nor in the case of the kid, common fodder. Let a human heart be born in them,

---

[52] The text has "in the first night," which does not suit the context.

80   The *Acts of Philip*

and they will follow us wherever we go, eating the same things we eat for your glory, and that they might speak like human beings, glorifying your name."

20. And at that moment the animals rose up, both the leopard and the kid, lifted up their forefeet and glorified God, and said with human voices: "We glorify and bless you, you who have visited us and remembered us in this wilderness, you who have transformed our savage and wild nature into tameness, and freely given us the divine word and placed in us a tongue and a mind so that we might speak and confess your name, because your glory is great."

21. After these words the leopard and the kid of the goat fell to the ground on their faces, paying homage to Philip and Bartholomew and Mariamne. At that moment the apostles glorified God and resolved that the kid and the leopard should journey together with them and go in front to the city to which they were going, just as the Savior revealed to them. So they went along together, praising and glorifying God, amen.

The Ninth Act
Concerning the Destruction of the Dragon[53]

1. Now the apostles were journeying along with one another—Philip and Bartholomew and Mariamne and the leopard and the kid—and they proceeded on the way for five days. After midnight prayers, early in the morning on the way, suddenly a strong and dark wind blew, and from its darkness a huge dark dragon charged up on the servants of God. Its back was blackened, but its belly was like charcoal, glowing bronze with sparks of fire, and its body stretched out more than a hundred cubits. A multitude of serpents and a multitude of their offspring were following it. And for a long time[54] the whole area of the wilderness was shaking.

2. At this sight Philip said to Bartholomew and Mariamne: "Now we need help from the Savior. Let us remember the word of Christ who sent us, saying: 'Fear nothing! Neither persecution, nor the serpents of that region, nor the shadowy dragon.' Let us therefore stand just as columns set firmly before God, and all the enemy's power will come to naught, and his threat will fail. So let us pray and purify the air with the cup, and this shadowy one will be stopped and the smoke will be suppressed."

---

[53] We continue to follow *Vaticanus graecus 824* (V).
[54] Or in a spatial sense, "over a large area," or "the whole place."

3. So after taking their cup, they prayed in this way: "You are the one who dampens every fire and abates darkness and puts a bit in the mouth of the dragon, the one who renders his anger impotent, who turns back the evil of the hostile stranger and drowns him in his own fire, who shuts his lair and bars his ways out and slaps his arrogance. Come among us in this wilderness, for we run by your will and by your command."

4. And turning, Philip said to Bartholomew and Mariamne: "Now rise, lift up your hands with the cup that we hold, and sprinkle in the air the sign of the cross, and see the glory of the powerful one."

5. Immediately there was a flash of fire and it blinded the dragon and the beasts with it. The dragon and the serpents were dried up at once, and the rays of light went into the openings of their dens and shattered the eggs of the serpents. But the apostles covered their eyes, since they were not able to look straight at the wonder of the flash of light. And so they passed through unharmed, proceeding on their way, praising our Lord Jesus Christ, amen.

[THE TENTH ACT OF THE HOLY APOSTLE PHILIP . . .][55]

[THE ELEVENTH ACT OF THE HOLY APOSTLE PHILIP . . .][56]

Xenophontos 32 (A)

1. ". . . in the wilderness places your sweetness remains with us and all who are firmly set on you."[57] After he said these things, Bartholomew and Mariamne were about to partake of the communion of the Savior. After calling out the amen, they glorified God, since they had been strengthened by a fast of five days to praise worthily, having become worthy of the fellowship of Christ.

2. And while Philip and Bartholomew and Mariamne were rejoicing, suddenly an earthquake and a clamor and a seething sounded from the place close by where there happened to be a great amount of broken

---

[55] The Tenth Act does not survive in any manuscript. In *Xenophontos 32* there is a lacuna of twenty-four folios (i.e., forty-eight pages) that corresponds to most of Act 8 as well as Acts 9 and 10 and part of Act 11.

[56] The title of Act 11 is lost (see the previous note).

[57] The text of *Xenophontos 32* (A) is rejoined (see notes 43 and 55) at what appears to be the end of a prayer by Philip.

stones. And from there voices were emerging in confusion and saying: "Depart from here from this point on, servants of the ineffable God. Attend to your business as we also attend to ours. How long will you be against us, wishing to obliterate the entire demonic nature? No one has ever passed by this place whom we have not[58] destroyed; against you alone we have become powerless. We are fifty demons of one nature who have obtained this small place as our portion. But you servants of Christ after passing through every place under heaven have come for our destruction, and this Jesus with you, who is the son of God, though he is only one, has obliterated countless kinds of demons. And now look, we are abandoning this cave, being cast out by force. We acknowledge from this point on that we have been brought to nothing, for the one who was crucified in opposition to us has destroyed[59] our ancient nature."

3. The apostle said: "I call on you by the crucified one that you display what your ancient nature is." And the dragon who was among them answered: "My nature originates from the plotting in paradise, and there he cursed me, the one who now wishes to destroy me through you. For at that time, after I withdrew from the lush garden, I found an opportunity to lurk in Cain because of Abel. Then when I displayed feminine beauty for the angels, I threw them down from the heights. And the women gave birth to very large sons—they call all these the Watchers.[60] And when these increased in number, they were devouring human beings like locusts. And after the flood wiped them out, they engendered the demonic and serpent-like nature when the rod of Moses exposed the nature of the Egyptian sages and magicians. For we are the fifty serpents that Moses' large serpent devoured at that time. Anyway, you, Philip, have seized victory over us."

4. Then the apostle, slave of God, looked toward heaven and said: "Holy Jesus, abode of unshaded light, glory of the Father, power of the powerless, timeless Word in the Father who also appeared on earth as a human being, come now and grant me strength, because a multitude of demons is inflicting indignities on your creatures in this wilderness. Do not delay, Master, but make haste with your aid." And as he was praying in this manner he cried out loudly and said: "I adjure you by the

---

[58] "Not" has been added as required by the context.

[59] Lit., "dried up"; see 11.5.

[60] "They call these the Watchers" is our conjecture for this crux where the Greek manuscript does not make sense.

glorified name of the Father, of the only-begotten Son, of the Most High, show yourselves, you demons, of what sort you are, both your number and your form." Immediately a very great screaming and disturbance came forth: "Take flight now, you descendants of darkness and bitterness, quickly on account of our inevitable and imminent destruction."

5. And when the demons, who had the appearance of reptiles, came out from the seething of the stones, fifty serpents having raised their heads ten feet high (for they were each more than sixty feet long), they were saying with one voice: "Approach, you who have commanded us to come out, for we are children of your nature." Then there was such a tremendous earthquake that Bartholomew and Mariamne would have lost courage had not Philip strengthened them, saying: "Whoever you are, the one being called by the serpents, which are evil demons, come forth, you on account of whom the earthquake has happened, since already you have been defeated and all your stock has dried up." Immediately a great dragon stood in the midst of the serpents, about a hundred cubits long, covered with soot and spewing out fire and pouring out much poison in a bursting torrent. It had a twenty-foot-long beard and a head like the peak of a mound of iron, swaying backward and forward, and a body completely like fire.

6. He raised himself to a great height and said to Philip: "Philip, son of thunder, what is this great authority that you possess so as to pass through this place against us? Why have you worked so hard to destroy me also, like the dragon in the wilderness? I implore you by the one who has granted you this authority, do not destroy us or obliterate us in the thunder of your anger. Send us into the mountains of the Labyrinth that we might lurk there and transform ourselves. And by our demonic power, in the same way as we served our lord Solomon the just in Jerusalem—for it was with our assistance that he built the sanctuary of God—so now also let us serve you. And in six days let us prepare for you in this place a building, and it shall be called the church of the living God. And I will even permit seven immortal springs because of the name of the crucified one, only do not destroy us."

7. The apostle replied: "How will you be able to build since you have a creeping nature and in fact are serpents, inasmuch as every building is fabricated by human skill? Now by the power of Jesus I command you, that both you and these fifty serpents change your creeping kind and display a human form." The dragon said: "Listen, Philip, our nature is shadowy and dark, and our father is called Darkness and our mother

Blackness. And they have brought us into the world as dark and black, with small feet, crooked hair, without knees, legs like the wind, airborne, with sparkling eyes, pointed beards, pointed hair, odious beings, mad for women, a mix of male and female." Then after sighing very deeply, the dragon said: "Philip, since you have become so strong, look upon our form." And immediately when the dragon and the fifty serpents revealed themselves as they are, they flew up like winds and cried out: "Let us now produce the building!" There was an interval of not quite three hours and they conveyed through the air fifty high columns and said: "Establish the place, Philip, as you wish, and you will see the building and the seven springs and the consecration of the church on the sixth day."

8. After six days the church was completed and streams were flowing like rivers. And in a few more days men, three thousand in number, and many women and infants were gathering together and they were magnifying Christ. And the dragon, showing himself even darker than an Ethiopian, said: "We are departing, Philip, to a place where we will no longer be seen by you, lest even there you command us to build. It suffices for us; we have been defeated."

9. Philip raised his voice—not the voice of the body, but that of the soul—and was speaking in his own language in the reasoning of the mind: "We glorify you: the inexpressible, the true, the precious and glorious offering. You are the bread, the glory of the Father, the grace of the Spirit, the garment of the Word purified and justified forever, the wealth being praised by many who do not know you, the one who gives life. You are the offspring of the Father, the one who is bound together with all until you release the one who has been bound, the one who does not eat and eats and is eaten, the one who offers the hearing of the word, the one who needs to receive the bath though he himself is the bath, the one who dances among the virgins, a dozen in number, and for him they sing praises in the Eighth of the Fullness, the one who adorns and is adorned, the one who sojourns and the one without a place, though he himself is all things, the holy temple that they wished to defile in the temple of abominations, where there is joy, the festal gathering that everyone longs for, the lamp that illuminates the house, and you yourself are the light. You are paradise, the mystery that dwells in silence, the intelligence of the one who dances in him, the couch of those who take their rest. You are the Word of the Father, the image of the truth, the one whom we have known and beheld. You are the hearing that hears with

our ears. You are the one who sees with our eyes, upon whom we have fixed our souls."

10. After he said these things Philip again distributed communion to Bartholomew and to Mariamne, and they glorified God for the communion of God, saying with great joy: "Amen, amen, amen."

The Twelfth Act of Saint Philip
When the Leopard and the Kid of the Goat Beg for Communion

1. Now when the apostle Philip had distributed communion to Bartholomew and Mariamne and while they were rejoicing, glorifying God, the leopard and the kid of the goat, as they watched them, were crying exceedingly and grieving in their own tongue. And their tears were flowing upon their jaws because they had not been considered worthy of the holy communion. And Philip said to Bartholomew: "I want to know why they are crying."

2. As Philip was saying this, the leopard opened its mouth, saying: "Servants of the First and the Only One, apostles of the divine greatness, I implore you by God, whose name came to us even though we were unworthy, that you not trouble yourselves over why we are crying. Instead I will speak on behalf of myself and the kid, and I will defend our grief. For since we were unreasoning beasts, we were living in ignorance until the day on which we saw you. I was eating flesh and blood, and the darkness of night was to me as light as noon. And when day broke, I would hide myself in the woods. But at the moment in which you were passing through the mountain, fear and trembling came upon us. And my savage nature was altered and transformed to goodness, and I held off from eating this kid, and the power of God was upon us.

3. "And now we are crying because you have not considered us worthy of the communion of Christ. We have spoken as human beings and beseeched God through you, in order that we might follow you. And it happened for us from God. And when in the uproar of the power of the dragon the only-begotten one appeared to you and the beauty of his form killed that dragon and the serpents, he did not exclude us from his mystery or the wonder of his face. But we heard his voice, and we also heard the glory of your prayers and blessings.

4. "If, therefore, God considered us worthy to participate in all of these marvels, why now do you not consider us worthy to receive communion? This is why we are crying in distress, because we have not been considered worthy. And if this is appropriate for me because I am

a wild beast, why would this kid not be worthy of communion? This is why we are crying, for perhaps we do not have life with God. Therefore have mercy on us, as you have been commanded, without envy, since he himself is in everyone, because he has given us the word[61] without envy. And this is a great wonder, that we, a wild beast and a goat's kid, have forsaken our own nature and become like human beings, and truly God lives in us. Now we beseech you, apostles of the good Savior, in order that you might freely grant to us without hesitation this part that we still lack, and that our beast-like bodies might be transformed by you and we might forsake the animal form.

5. "For we believe that this will come about for us through you, since the mind, which is within all reasonings and even within the heart, is indispensable. And behold it lived with us and guided us to precious perceptions. And in awakening us by its sleepless reason from the burden of wildness it changes us to tameness little by little, until we have become completely human in both body and soul. And we shall be in harmony with one another, in order that we might be considered worthy of the bread, the glorious mystery of which we have heard. Wherefore we ask you to receive this marvelous thing of glory from God, who watches over every nature, even that of wild animals, on account of his great compassion."

6. When the leopard had said these things on his own behalf and that of the kid, they were both crying. Then the apostle replied: "Listen to me, you animals who have become worthy so that the word of God has reached you. For this is clear, that God has visited all creation through his Christ, providing not only for human beings but also for the domestic animals and all the varieties of animals. Who can tell of his good providence, which works incessantly in us?"

7. And at that moment Philip raised his hands and prayed, saying: "My Lord Jesus Christ, the hope and power of all, the king of glory, the one who made the heavens, the one who secured the abyss and condemned the enemy to it, the one who stretched out the firmament and set the stars in it for the glory of your works, the one who arranged the air for the enjoyment and breath of those who need it, the one who gave his sweetness to the waters for the life of your creation, the one who rebuked the sea and stilled the waters, you are the Lord of all lofty knowledge, the liberty of those in bondage, the savior of the ages, the

---

[61] Or, perhaps, "he has given us speech."

one who heals those blinded by the opaque spots of evil. Come, our Lord Jesus Christ, if it is your will, and just as you changed the form of the soul of these animals, so make them appear to themselves in the bodily appearance of human beings, for the glory and honor of your name, in the place to which we are going."

8. And Philip took the cup and filled it with water, and he sprinkled it upon them. And at that moment, little by little, the forms of their faces and bodies were transformed into the likenesses of human beings. And they stood upon their feet and stretched out their forefeet in the place of hands and glorified God, speaking in this way: "We glorify you, Lord, the only begotten Son, on account of the undying life into which we have been born, having received in place of an animal body a human one. Truly you are the genuine judge of those who approach you, you who have granted us today the glorious word in order to make us associates of your evangelists. For you have stripped off our beastly uncleanness and clothed us with the gentleness of the saints. We praise you and bless you, because you have brought us from the absence of glory into glory. We believe that there is no life among either creature or human being unless God should visit for our salvation."

The Thirteenth Act of the Holy Apostle Philip
The Arrival in Hierapolis

1. Now the apostles were traveling toward the city, and with them two animals who appeared to themselves as human beings. And Philip was signaling to the leopard so that he would lead them on the way to the city. And when they reached the peak of the mountain, they looked down and saw lying on the slope the city to which the Lord had sent them. While they were looking down, they saw men before the city and said to one another: "Let us go to these men and ask the name of the city." And as they proceeded, the men saw them and moved to encounter them. Now everyone in that region had a serpent on his shoulders, and they would receive signs from them. And they were asking the serpents: "Who are these people coming toward us?" This was how the sign worked for them. They would release the serpents upon the strangers, and if they were not bitten by them they were shown to them as participating in the same abomination. But if they were bitten by the serpents, they were seen as their enemies and they did not permit them to enter into the city.

2. When the apostles approached to speak to these men, who were seven in number, each of them let down his own serpent. And the serpents bowed their heads to the ground before the apostles and remained there, biting their own tongues. And the men concluded that they also worshipped the Viper. So Philip went on his way with the others. And the men of that region were intent on the animals following them and speaking as people, and they were astonished.

3. When they reached the city limits, behold, there were two large dragons in front of the city gate, one on the right and one on the left, keeping watch lest any stranger enter this city. For by breathing upon them they would blind their eyes. As the apostles were entering, the dragons raised their heads, and when they saw them at the gate they were roaring to one another. But when Philip looked toward them, they saw the ray of the light of the Monad shining in his eyes, and in that moment they turned their heads aside and they died.

4. Once they had entered the city, the apostles found a vacant clinic near the gate in which no doctor was established. And Philip said to Mariamne: "Look, our Master had preceded us and prepared for us this spiritual clinic. So let us stay in it and we shall find rest, because we have become weary from the rigors of the road." Next he said to Bartholomew: "Where is the box that the Savior gave us at the time we were in Galilee? Let us get established in this clinic and take care of the sick, until we discern the plan that the Savior will arrange for us."

5. Then Philip opened his mouth and spoke in this way: "The living voice of the Most High has visited us, and with it we destroy the rulers of the world of darkness and take away the hardness of humanity. Let us cure the malady of the blind, and exorcize the demons of forgetfulness and cast them out from this dwelling place in which we reside. Blessed is the one who has received in himself this gospel, for this one is the light of the blind that is visible in the mind's eye, which is Christ. For he is the eye of the one who cannot be contemplated, the face of the invisible, the glory of the impalpable, the structure of the infinite, the way to the unapproachable, the victory of the one who contends well, the prize of those who run, the joy of those who toil and wait for him, the knowledge of the ignorant, the endurance of the long suffering, the rest of the afflicted, the salvation of the lost, the freedom of the enslaved, the service of those in need, the possession of the poor, the abundance of the hungry. King of those who serve as soldiers, you are the leader and Lord of every creature, the supper of the elect, the private

room of those who pray, the dwelling place of those who withdraw from the world,[62] the city of those who know him. He is the one who became lamb and sheep and shepherd, the author of life. To him be glory and power and authority over everything, amen." And the apostles and the animals cried out, "Amen!"

THE FOURTEENTH ACT OF THE HOLY APOSTLE PHILIP CONCERNING STACHYS THE BLIND

1. Now there happened to be near that place the house of a rich man named Stachys, who had been blind for forty years. When he heard Philip saying these things as he sat by his window, he wept before his children and said: "Help me and take me to those people residing at the gate, for they are able to heal my eyes and grant me light." His sons said to him: "Who are those physicians?" And Stachys said to them: "They are men residing at the gate whom I heard saying: 'Let us settle in this clinic and let us heal every suffering and every disease.'"

2. So after the sons with his slaves rose and took hold of his hands, they led him to the apostles. And after he fell upon the ground and was prostrate before them, he said: "I call upon you, strangers who have come to this city, certainly for my sake and because of the disability[63] which is in me, in order that I also may be cured. Look, for three days I've had dreams, seeing astounding things, although I have not seen the light of the sun for forty years. Before I was blinded, I was a persecutor of strangers and Christians. And I was presiding over all those devoted to the cult of the Viper and the serpents, which were near my house on the street called Ophioryme; for everyone in the city venerates the serpents.

3. "And it came about as I was lying in bed with my eyes open and looking at the ceiling of my bedroom, I saw serpents' eggs, and from these eggs newborn serpents were leaping out. And my mind was stirred and I said: 'Are these then gods?' I will take a little liquid from the serpents' eggs and put it on my eyes in order that I might see whether they are in some way therapeutic. But when I put the substance from the eggs on my eyes, they were struck with an inflammation that lasted for ten whole years. At that time my wife was still alive and she used to go to the

---

[62] The Greek expression here, τῶν ἀναχωρητῶν, "of those who withdraw," is a technical term for monks, particularly for hermits. We have added the phrase "from the world" to communicate the intended sense.

[63] Note that πήρωσις frequently means "blindness."

mountain and would bring me dew from the plants and put it each day on my eyes, and I was relieved. But one day after she rose early she was going to the mountain in order to bring me dew, and an immense beast charged up and struck her. And she expired from this blow because there was no physician to treat her. And from that time until now I have not seen light, nor have I seen the face of my sons.

4. "Therefore I call upon you, man of God, to cure me of this ordeal and I will believe in God through you, because my vision is true. For I saw myself with a towel bound over my eyes; indeed, the one I serve is himself the one who covers my face and prevents me from seeing the light. Then a voice called me, saying: 'Stachys, come to the city gate and you will find there the physician and he will grant you light, and then you will know that the one you serve is the devil.' So I went to the place by the gate, and when I looked up with my eyes I saw a likeness of a handsome young man with three faces: the first face had the form of a young man who did not yet have a beard; the middle face had the form of a woman clothed in a glorious garment; and the third face had the form of an old man. There was a water pitcher on the young man's shoulder, and the young woman had a torch in her hand and my eyes were filled with light from that torch. And all those in the city came and were being baptized by the young man who carried the water pitcher, and the bodies of those being baptized became white like the white branches of palm trees. I saw this dream three times in the same way. Therefore I beg you, do not restrain the healing of this man whose soul has lingered in darkness, for I believe that God is the one who has revealed himself to me. Therefore let your help come upon me, so that I will regain my sight."

5. When Philip heard these words of Stachys, he raised his voice, saying: "Blessed be your name, O good Jesus. You who send us in every place like sheep, you are our true shepherd, you who edify our nature and govern all things in righteousness. You sent us here as strangers and in anticipation you prepared our dwelling place. We were as humble people and miserable and without a place among other people. But you by your good foresight planted a paradise for us, O perfect man and perfect one from heaven, the one who has the unutterable name, the saving right hand, whose name cannot be spoken by lips which form an impure instrument, the great Spirit, the one who is most highly exalted among your bright aeons, the Father who is in secret, the one who is with us in three perfect forms, which are images of the invisible, the one who is blessed forever, amen."

6. Then, after this, he stretched out his right hand and took hold of Stachys, saying: "Attach yourself to me, you who have lingered in your blindness on account of your ignorance. For what you have seen is true; so do not call it a dream, because dreams are only prodigies, but this vision is from the Holy Spirit. Until now you were bound by Satan; he is the one who is carrying off all of humanity with his death-bringing potions, which he pours into souls, making their minds dark and not allowing them to see the heavenly glory, but rather leading humanity through forgetfulness into the ruin of corruption. From birth people are seized by ignorance, and as their bodies grow little by little they are intoxicated by forgetfulness and submerged first in the error of fornication, then in idolatry, and in wrath, and in anger, and in hatred, and in slander. It is ignorance that perverts toward all evil works; it makes the mind dim; it blinds people; darkness and night are the diadem of ignorance. Now recognize that the one who calls you gives you the true light, in order that by it you might know that the one you have served in the past was the devil; because he is the one who made you blind during all this time."

7. And after he drew him near to himself, Philip stretched out his hand and dipped his finger in Mariamne's mouth and smeared [. . .][64] and he held a great reception for them and boiled for them a stew from the beasts of the field and filtered fine wine for them.[65]

8. And talk of it spread through the whole city and some were saying: "Come and see the reverent people, one of whom opened Stachys' eyes after he had not seen light for forty years. Surely a power of God is present with them, since the skill of human physicians is not able to effect such a great cure." A large crowd gathered at his house on account of Philip and those who were with him, and everyone was running to see those who were sick and the demon possessed being healed; and the jaundiced and the dropsical were being cured.

9. Philip was baptizing the men and Mariamne the women, and all the crowds were exceedingly amazed because the leopard and the kid of the goat were pronouncing the amen. And there was great confusion in

---

[64] The length of the lacuna here is one folio (two sides of a page).

[65] The diet of stew and fine wine is somewhat surprising (see also note 69), given the emphasis elsewhere on the ascetic profile (see note 62).

every place and in the multitude, among the great and the small and the rich and the poor, in those days. And to our God. . . .[66]

THE FIFTEENTH ACT OF THE HOLY APOSTLE PHILIP CONCERNING NICANORA, THE GOVERNOR'S WIFE

1. Now there was a governor in that city called Tyrannognophos,[67] and he had a wife named Nicanora, a native of Syria. While traveling by sea, she had been thrown overboard[68] by the gusting wind and was driven inland to that city. And because she was rich, Tyrannognophos took her as his wife. But the city serpents used to bite her as a stranger, and her body was stricken from their venom and she remained in constant torment. When she heard that Stachys had regained his sight, she asked to be taken by her servants to Stachys' house; and they took her without the knowledge of her husband. Now the apostles were inside the house, being attended to by Stachys.

2. The apostle Philip said to Stachys: "Stachys, you who previously were bound by the false power of Satan and for a very long time remained in the blindness in which you used to suffer day after day until yesterday, know now that God did not leave you until the end in the ignorance and error in which you stood. But you received the true medicine from the good Father. And the sun of righteousness has risen in your house, bringing its shining and glorious rays into your courtyard. Accordingly, do not indulge in the delicacies of domestic animals, lest you be reckoned with the wild beasts; do not delight in much wine, since it leads astray to idols; do not boast in silver and gold, because they are snares of Satan. But rather be firm in faith, and with a heart full of reverence welcome for yourself continence and discipline, because continence is the support of everything. This is the wealth of God.

3. "Look, the peace of God has taken root in your house. Do not be ignorant from this day forward, that you might not turn aside to the worse. And the seal of the Spirit will dwell with you. Hold yourself upright as a pillar in the church of truth and live, Stachys, in continence, because sanctity abolishes all lawlessness. For sanctity is the bridge for

---

[66] Act 14 ends abruptly. The text may have been shortened. Perhaps we should add δόξα to yield "And glory to our God!"

[67] The name, which means "tyrant of darkness," signifies the governor's frightening character.

[68] Or, alternatively, "shipwrecked."

the souls of the righteous, and it abolishes the source of corruption. Therefore, raise yourself above the pollution of desire. Do not allow meat eating and excessive drinking of wine to rule in your members, lest your soul be cast in that mold. Cleanse yourself from fornication, because this is ruin, the bride of death, the wedding of destruction, the joy of demons, the exultation of uncleanness, the delight of envy, the enjoyment of those who are corrupting themselves. Abide rather in love, and be prudent knowing Christ spiritually, and reject for yourself honor in this life, and seek heavenly glory. Let your sons be useful and your daughters virgins, and let your servants be taught continence. For your house will be called a house of prayer and you yourself will be delivered from confusion and turmoil."

4. And after he said these things he planted his staff in Stachys' courtyard and prayed in this way: "Lord Jesus Christ, the true staff, the life-giving way, in your name let this rod sprout just like the rod of Aaron. And let it become a great plant and tree, and let it be a sign and a means of healing for the sick for all generations." And it sprouted immediately and became a laurel tree, with the result that Stachys and all the others marveled at this incredible sign.

5. And he was taking thought for the poor, having filled three large jars with grain, wine, and olive oil. And he was giving to the crowd from unfailing provisions even though no one was refilling the jars, and he was providing for the poor until the day of Stachys' departure.[69]

6. When Nicanora heard the apostle's words and about the signs that he did at the house of Stachys, she forgot her disease owing to the joy that seized her because of the word of God. But her servants said to her: "Our Lady, you know do you not that your husband Tyrannognophos is a harsh man? If he learns that we have brought you here without his knowledge, he will maltreat us. So let us go back to our home before he departs from the court, lest he subject to torture those who are practicing healing in Stachys' house on account of you." When she heard the word of her servants, she returned to the house of Tyrannognophos overcome with grief and saying: "It is better for me to remain in the torment and threat of the serpents than to become the cause of trouble for the servants of God."

---

[69] The subject here seems to be Philip, though it is strange for him to be providing wine and oil (see note 65).

94 The *Acts of Philip*

7. And she was by herself during the night praying to God, saying: "Lord Jesus Christ, hear my supplication and grant me the request which I am asking from you, my God. You are high over all and have power over all. For nothing is impossible for you, but you answer all those who petition you in truth. For I ask from you neither gold nor silver, but I am enduring the disease of the body and the strikes of the serpents; for these are small things, if you grant me rest for my soul. The harassment of the serpents is nothing, if I should hear your words. Therefore, I beseech you, in order that Tyrannognophos might believe in you or die, since he prevents me from going to your holy apostles. My Lord Jesus, grant me an opportunity that I might go to them, or they come to me. Only make me a participant of your holy word, because this is the true physician, healing not only the body, but also the soul." [. . .][70] "they exist, for this reason you see visions; for you cannot deceive me, like the wives who mock their husbands. But if I should learn that you have gone to them, I will take vengeance on them and I will shut you in a dark place. Therefore, choose the will of your heart, for I will be keeping a close eye on them, especially on account of you." And when he left her, he went to his tribunal.

8. Now Philip and Bartholomew and Mariamne and the leopard and the kid of the goat were in the house of Stachys, in Christ Jesus our Lord, to whom be glory and power as well as to the Father together with the Holy Spirit, now and always and forever and ever, amen.

FROM THE TRAVELS OF THE HOLY AND MOST BLESSED APOSTLE PHILIP
FROM ACT FIFTEEN, IN WHICH THE MARTYRDOM IS FOUND[71]

Vaticanus graecus 824 (V)

1. During that time, when the emperor Trajan had taken dominion over the Romans, in the eighth year of his reign, after Simon the son of

---

[70] A lacuna of one folio interrupts; the manuscript picks up at the end of a discourse by Tyrannognophos.

[71] The *Xenophontos 32* (A) manuscript has a new title at the beginning of the *Martyrdom*. This probably means that the scribe at this point followed a different model of the *Acts of Philip* from that utilized for Acts 1–15. This model represents a shorter form (designated recension Θ) in comparison to the one (designated recension Γ) attested by the Vatican manuscript (V). Consequently we translate from the longer text of *Vaticanus graecus 824* (V). There is a third recension designated Δ, but it has not yet been properly edited.

Clopas, who was bishop of Jerusalem, was martyred, having been the second bishop of that church after James, who was called brother of the Lord, Philip the apostle, as he was passing through the cities and regions of Lydia, proclaimed to all the gospel of Christ.

2. And when he reached the city of Ophioryme, which is called Hierapolis of Asia, he was welcomed by a certain believer named Stachys. Bartholomew, one of the seventy disciples of the Lord, was with him, and his sister Mariamne and his disciples who were following him. Many men and women had assembled at the house of Stachys, and Philip together with Bartholomew was teaching them the things concerning Jesus.

3. Philip's sister Mariamne, sitting at the entrance of the house of Stachys, was paying attention to those who were approaching, persuading them to give a hearing to the apostles, who were saying to them: "Our brothers and sisters, children of the Father who is in heaven, you are the beautiful riches and the actuality of the city above, the delight of the dwelling place which God has prepared for those who love him.

4. "Trample down the snares of the enemy and the coiling serpent. For his way is crooked, since he is a son of the evil one and there is in him an evil poison. Indeed, his father is the devil, the agent of death, and his mother corruption. There is wrath in his eyes and destruction in his mouth and his way is Hades. Therefore, flee from him, the one who does not have substance, the amorphous one who alone does not have a form in all creation, whether in heaven or on earth, whether among the birds or among the beasts. For all things turn away from his form. For among the beasts and the birds of heaven his nakedness is singular, because the serpent trails along on his belly and chest. Death is his dwelling place, even Tartaros, and he walks in darkness since he does not have confidence in anything. So flee from him, lest his poison pour out upon your mouth.

5. "But rather become faithful, doers of good, free from deceit. Root out the evil system from yourselves, namely, the desires of wickedness, through which the serpent, the evil dragon, the author of evil has produced the food of destruction and death for the soul, since every desire of wicked things comes originally from him and this desire is the root of lawlessness, the system of wicked things, the death of souls. For the desire of the enemy arms itself against the faithful. It comes out from the darkness and proceeds in the darkness, endeavoring to wage war upon those who are in the light. For this is the beginning of covetousness.

6. "Therefore, you who are willing to come to us—actually God has become present through us to you, to show you mercy and deliver you from the evil snare of the enemy—flee the wicked desires of the enemy and expel them completely from your mind by openly hating the father of wicked things and loving Jesus, who is light and life and truth and savior of all of those who long for him. So when you run up to him, hold fast to him in love so that he might lead you out of the pit of wicked things and, after he has cleansed you, establish you as blameless and living in truth before his Father."

7. Now Philip was saying these things to the gathered multitudes because from time immemorial they revered the serpents and the Viper, whose images they set up and worshiped. And for this reason they also used to call Hierapolis, Ophioryme. While Philip was saying these things, Bartholomew, Mariamne, his disciples, and Stachys were present with him, and the entire people listened. And a great multitude of them who had escaped from the enemy turned to the Lord and were added to Philip and those around him. And the faithful were further strengthened in the love of Christ.

8. Now Nicanora, the wife of the proconsul, as she was lying in bed, suffering from various ailments, especially of the eyes, heard news about the apostle Philip and his preaching and she believed in Jesus. Indeed, she had been hearing about him for some time, and when she called upon his name she was delivered from the pains afflicting her. And she rose up and went out of her house by the side door. She was carried by her own slaves in a silver litter and went to the house of Stachys, where the apostles were.

9. When she arrived in front of the entrance to the house, Mariamne, the sister of Philip the apostle, saw her and spoke to her in the Hebrew language in front of Philip and Bartholomew and all the multitude of those who had believed, saying: "Daughter of the Father, you are my mistress. You were given as a pledge to the serpent. But Jesus our redeemer has come to break through your bonds and cut them and pluck them out from you by their roots, because you are my sister—one mother brought us forth as twins. You have forgotten your father; you have forgotten the path leading to the dwelling place of your mother, being in error. You have forsaken that temple of the deceit of temporary glory and come to us, having fled the enemy, because he is the dwelling place of death. Now behold your redeemer has come that he might

redeem you. The sun of righteousness, Christ, has dawned upon you that he might enlighten you."

10. When Nicanora heard these things as she stood before the doors, she gained confidence and cried out and said before all: "I am a Hebrew and a daughter of Hebrews. Speak with me in the language of my ancestors. For when I heard the preaching of my ancestors, I was cured immediately of my disease and the pains encompassing me. Therefore I prostrate myself before the goodness of God, because he made you take the trouble to come as far as this city for the sake of his true and precious stone, that through you we might receive his knowledge and live with you having believed in him."

11. When Nicanora had said these things, the apostle Philip prayed for her to God together with Bartholomew and Mariamne and those with them, saying: "You who give life to the dead, Christ Jesus, Master, you who have set us free through baptism from slavery to death, deliver her completely from the error of the enemy. Grant life to her in your perfection, that she might enter into the land of her ancestors in freedom, having a share in your goodness, Lord Jesus."

12. Now when all had pronounced the amen together with the apostle Philip, suddenly Tyrannos, Nicanora's husband, arrived like an untamed and enraged horse. And when he had seized his wife's garments, he was crying out, saying: "Nicanora, did I not leave you lying on your bed? How then did you have such strength to come to these magicians? And how were you relieved from the inflammation of your eyes? Now then if you do not tell me who your doctor is and what his name is, I will punish you with various punishments and I will not have mercy upon you."

13. And she answered saying to him: "Tyrannos, cast off from yourself this tyranny of yours and forget this evil of yours, forsake this temporary life, put away the beastly quality of your vile mind, flee the cruel dragon and his desires, throw off from yourself the instruments and the bite of the homicidal serpent, keep away from the foul and accursed evils of idols, evils which are fields of the enemy and a dark wall. Rather acquire for yourself an honorable and spotless life, that when you are found in holiness you might be able to know my physician and accept his name. So if you wish me to remain by your side, prepare yourself well to remain in purity and continence and in fear of the true God, and I will live together with you for all time. Cleanse yourself from the idols and all their filth."

14. When Tyrannos, her husband, heard these words, he grabbed her hair and was dragging her and kicking her, and he said: "It is better for you to die by the sword than for you to be seen by me fornicating with these magicians. For I see that you have fallen under the spell of these deceivers. Therefore I will kill you first in a cruel manner, and then not sparing these others, after I have cruelly mocked them, I will slay them in a most abusive way." And he turned and said to those around him: "Bring me the magicians, those impostors." So after the executioners ran into the house of Stachys and seized Philip and Bartholomew and Mariamne, they were dragging them along, leading them to the place where the proconsul was. And the most faithful Stachys followed and all the faithful.

15. When the proconsul saw them he ground his teeth together and said: "Torture these magicians who have deceived many women and men, boys and girls, representing themselves as devotees, while they are, in fact, abominations." And he ordered rough leather straps to be brought and Philip, Bartholomew, and Mariamne to be beaten. And after they had been flogged with the straps, he ordered their feet to be bound and that they be dragged through the streets of the city as far as the gate of their temple. Large crowds gathered together so that almost no one remained at home, and they were all amazed at them because of their fortitude and endurance as they were violently and inhumanly dragged along.

16. And after the proconsul had tortured the saints around the apostle Philip, he ordered them to be brought and secured in the temple of the idol of the Viper. But the saints were being strengthened in the faith of Christ, exalting in the endurance of the saints. And together all with one voice were glorifying God, saying the amen.

17. When the apostle Philip and Bartholomew and Mariamne had been shut in the temple of the Viper, the priests of the Viper gathered together in the same place and a large crowd of about seven hundred men, and they ran to the proconsul and were crying out, saying: "Avenge us against these strangers, these magicians, these seducers who have led the people astray. For from the time they settled among us, our city has been full of every evil deed. They even killed the serpents, the children of our goddess. They also shut the temple and the altar is abandoned, and we have not found any wine offered to the Viper, so that after drinking it, she might sleep. If you wish to know that these people are really magicians, look and see how they wish to enchant us, saying: 'Live in

purity and holiness, once you have believed in God'; how they entered the city; how the dragons did not blind them; how they did not drink their blood, but rather these dragons, who guard our city from every stranger, were struck down by them!"

18. When the proconsul heard these things he was even more inflamed with anger; he was filled with wrath and threat and being exceedingly angry he said to the priests: "What! Have they enchanted my wife? Since that time she says strange things to me and she is praying all through the night, illuminated by a strange light and groaning deeply, saying: 'Jesus, the true light, has come to me.' So when I went out from my bedroom, I wished to spy out through the window and see whom she was calling, 'Jesus, the light.' And something like a bright ray of light struck me, with the result that I was momentarily blinded;[72] and from that moment I was afraid of my wife because of her luminous Jesus. Tell me, priests, what should I do?" They said: "Proconsul, perhaps we are no longer priests; for since you shut them up, when they pray, not only has the temple been shaken, but perhaps it is also collapsing."

19. Then the proconsul commanded them to bring those around Philip out from the temple and bring them to the tribunal, saying to the executioners: "When you have stripped Philip and those with him of their clothing, search them for instruments of their magic." So they stripped Philip first and then Bartholomew. And they also came upon Mariamne and dragged her out and said: "Let us strip her naked so that all may see her, how being a woman she follows men, for she especially deceives all the women." And Tyrannos said to the nonpriests:[73] "Proclaim round about the city that everyone should come, men and women, so that they might see her shame, because she travels together with these magicians and is doubtless debauched by them." And he ordered Philip to be hung up and his ankles pierced through, and that iron instruments of torture be brought and passed through his heels, and that he be hung head downward before the temple on a tree. And after they stretched out Bartholomew facing Philip, they pinned his hands on the wall of the temple gate.

20. Philip and Bartholomew both smiled when they saw one another, since it was as if they were not being tortured, for their punishments

---

[72] Or, "I was almost blinded."

[73] The curious term "nonpriests" (also at *Mart.* 25) is probably a Christian terminological innovation to speak of priests of another religion; note the statement at the end of the preceding paragraph, "we are no longer priests."

were prizes and crowns. And when they stripped Mariamne, immediately the likeness of her body was changed in the presence of all. And there was a cloud of fire around her before them all, and they were completely unable to look toward the spot where Mariamne was, but they all fled from her.

21. Philip spoke to Bartholomew in the Hebrew language, saying: "Where is brother John? For look, I am being released from the body, and who will pray for us? Because they have even attacked our sister Mariamne in an inappropriate manner. And look, they have set fire to Stachys' house, saying: 'Let us burn it, since he welcomed them.' So are you willing, Bartholomew, that we might call down fire from heaven and burn them up?"

22. Just as Philip was saying these things, suddenly John entered into the city as though he were their fellow citizen. And as he moved about the main square he asked: "Who are these people and why are they being punished?" And they said to him: "Perhaps you are not from our city and that is why you ask about these people? They have wronged many, they have shut down our gods and by their magic they have destroyed the serpents and the dragons; but they have also raised many dead, who have terrified us by relating in full numerous punishments. Even while they are hanging there, these strangers wish to request fire from heaven and burn up both us and our city."

23. Then John said: "Let's go and you show them to me." So they led John as their fellow citizen to the spot where Philip was. And there was a large crowd around him, including the proconsul and the priests. And when Philip saw John, he said to Bartholomew in Hebrew: "Brother, John has come, the one who went to Barek where the living water is." And John saw Philip head downward, hanging from his ankles and heels; and he also saw Bartholomew stretched out on the temple wall and said to them: "The mystery of the one who was hung in the middle between heaven and earth, will be with you."

24. And he said to the people of that city: "People who dwell in Ophioryme Hierapolis, great is the ignorance which is among you. For you have been led astray on the way of error. By breathing, the dragon blew on you and blinded you in three ways, namely, he made you blind in body, blind in soul, and blind in spirit, and you were struck by the destroyer. Consider all of creation, whether on earth or in heaven or in the sea, and see that the serpent does not share any resemblance with human beings, but his race belongs to corruption and destruction and

has been abolished by God, and for this reason he is twisting and winding, and there is no life at all in him. Rather, there is wrath and anger and darkness and fire and smoke in his members. Now then, why are you punishing these people? Is it because they have said to you: 'The serpent is your enemy'?"

25. When they heard these words from John, they raised their hands against him, saying: "We thought you were our fellow citizen, but now you have made it evident that you are their partner. So in the same way as these you also will be put to death. For the priests have determined to squeeze out the blood of all of you and, after mixing it with wine, to offer it to the Viper to drink."

When the nonpriests attempted to seize John, their hands were paralyzed. And John said to Philip: "Let us not return evil for evil." And Philip said to John: "Look, it may be that my Lord Jesus told me not to avenge myself. Nevertheless, I will no longer hold myself back, but I will bring my full indignation upon them and destroy them all."

26. John and Bartholomew and Mariamne were trying to prevent him, saying: "Our teacher was beaten and whipped, gall and sour wine were given him to drink, and he said: 'Forgive them, for they do not know what they do.' And he also taught this, saying: 'Learn from me, because I am gentle and humble in heart.'" Philip said: "Keep away from me and do not try to calm me, because I will not put up with you, because they hung me head downward and pierced my ankles and heels with iron hooks. And you, beloved of God, John, see how much you discussed with them yet they did not pay attention to you. Therefore, yield to me and I will curse them and they will be utterly destroyed at once." And he began to curse them, calling upon the Lord and crying out in Hebrew: "Father of our Lord Jesus Christ, the only almighty God, before whom all shudder from eternity, the powerful and impartial judge, whose name is in your power, Sabaoth Ael. Blessed are you forever. Before you the rulers and authorities of heavenly power tremble, even the cherubim who stand in their fire-breathing fury. Holy king of majesty, whose name reached to the beasts of the wilderness and they became tame and praised you with a perceptible voice; you who look upon us and readily grant our requests; you who have known us before we were created; you, the overseer of all things; now I beseech you, let great Hades open his mouth and then the great abyss swallow up these godless people who have resolved not to make room for the word of truth in this city. Yes indeed, Sabaoth."

27. And then suddenly the abyss was opened and the whole place where the proconsul sat was swallowed up, along with the entire temple and the Viper that they were worshiping and the priests of the Viper, and about seven thousand men, not including women and children. Only the place where the apostles were remained unmoved. Even the proconsul was swallowed down into the abyss. And their voices were rising up from below with wailing, saying: "Have mercy on us, God of your glorious apostles, because now we see the punishments of those who have not confessed the crucified one. Look, the cross shines on us. Jesus Christ, show yourself, because we are all going down living into Hades and are being whipped because we have unjustly crucified your apostles." And a voice was heard, saying: "I will be merciful to you by my luminous cross."

28. But Stachys and all his house remained behind, along with the proconsul's wife and fifty other women who had believed with her on the Lord, and further a considerable number of men and women as well as one hundred virgins, who on account of their purity had not been swallowed up since they had been marked with the seal of Christ.

29. Then the Lord appeared to Philip and said: "Philip, did you not hear from me 'Do not return to anyone evil for evil'? Why have you struck such a multitude with destruction, Philip? Who having placed a hand on the plow and looking at what lies behind makes a straight furrow? or Who gives their lamp away to another and sits in darkness? or Who gives their house away to another and lives in a garbage pile? Who ignores their clothing in winter and goes about naked? or What enemy will rejoice in the joy of the one who hates him? and What slave who has completed his master's command will not be commended? and What soldier goes to battle without full armor? and Who runs excellently in the stadium and does not receive the prize? and Who having washed his clothes gladly stains them, Philip? Behold, my bridal chamber is prepared, and blessed is the one who is found in it with the bright garment; for this is the one who receives the crown upon his head. Behold, the supper is prepared, and blessed is the one who is invited and ready to come to the one who has invited him. Great is the harvest of the field, and blessed is the good laborer. See the lilies of the field and all the flowers; the good farmer is the first of those who share them. But how, Philip, have you become heartless, with the result that you have called down curses upon your enemies in anger?"

30. Philip said: "Why are you angry with me, Lord, that I called down curses upon my enemies? Indeed, why do you not strike them down since they still live in the abyss? You know, Lord, that it is on your account that I came into this city and in your name I drove out every error of the idols from it and all the demons. The dragons and the serpents withered. And since these people did not welcome your light, for this reason I cursed them and they went down into Hades alive."

31. The Savior said to Philip: "But since you disobeyed me and have returned evil for evil and have not kept my commandment, for this reason you will fulfill your destiny, gloriously to be sure, and be led by the hand by my holy angels to the paradise of delights. They will come to me in paradise, but you I will order to be barred outside of paradise for forty days, awed by the flaming and spinning sword. And you will groan from the bottom of your heart, because you maltreated those who maltreated you. But after forty days I will send my angel Michael and he will restrain the sword that guards paradise and you will see all the righteous who walked during their lives in innocence, and then you also will worship the glory of my Father who is in heaven. In any case the sign of your passing will be glorified by my cross. As for Bartholomew, after he departs for Lycaonia he will also be crucified there. And Mariamne, her body is to be placed in the Jordan River. But as for me, Philip, I will not tolerate you, because you swallowed up the people in the abyss. But behold my spirit is in them and I will lead them out of the abyss, and thus when they see you they will believe in the glory of the one who sent you."

32. The Savior turned and stretched out his hand and sketched out a cross in the air, coming down from the heights to the abyss. And the abyss was filled with light, and the cross took on the appearance of a ladder with steps. And the Savior called out with a loud voice into the abyss, saying: "Everyone come up by means of the cross, because the apostle now also has compassion for you on account of me, that you might again see the light of God." And behold the entire multitude of those who had been brought down into the abyss came back up; but the proconsul remained below and the Viper that they used to worship. And when the crowds came up, they looked at Philip and saw him hanging head downward, and they mourned with weeping and great lament at the lawless act that they had committed. They also saw Bartholomew and Mariamne restored to her earlier form.

Then the Lord ascended into the heavens, while Philip and Bartholomew and Mariamne and Stachys and all the faithful people watched; and in silence they were glorifying God with fear and trembling. And all the crowds cried out, saying: "There is one God, who sent these people for our salvation; there is one God, whom these people proclaim in truth. Now we truly repent for our great error, because we are not yet worthy of eternal life. Now we believe, because we have seen great wonders, because the Savior has led us up from the abyss." And they all fell on their faces and prostrated themselves before Philip and were calling on him because they were ready to flee from their error; and they were praying that they might become worthy of the presence of Christ.

33. Then Philip, still hanging there, addressed them and said: "Listen and learn how many are the powers of my God, remembering what you saw below and how your city was overturned except for the house of Stachys, who welcomed me; but now the tenderness of my God has led you up from the abyss. And I am under obligation to wander around outside of paradise for forty days on account of you, because I was angry with you to the point of retribution. And this commandment of my Lord alone I did not keep, because I did not give you good in exchange for evil. But I say to you, from now on, in the goodness of God, reject evil, that you may become worthy of the communion of the Lord."

34. And some of the faithful ran up so that they might take Philip down and remove the iron instruments of torture from him and the hooks from his ankles. But Philip said: "No, my children, do not approach me and this is why, because in this way my life will reach its fulfillment. Listen to me, you who have been enlightened in the Lord. I came into this city in the outward form you see. Therefore, do not grieve because I am hanging in this way. For I bear the type of the first human brought head downward upon the earth and once more being made alive through the cross of wood from the death caused by transgression. And now I am fulfilling what was assigned to me, for the Lord said to me: 'Unless you make your things below as the things above, and the things on the left as the things on the right,[74] you will not enter into my kingdom.' Therefore do not become like the type that has been changed into its opposite, because all the world has been changed and every soul dwelling in the body becomes forgetful of heavenly things. So let those

---

[74] Or, "Unless you conform what is below to what is above." There seem to be two basic options for understanding the sense here: (1) reversal/transformation or (2) adaptation/conformity. The meaning in either case may be paraphrased as "unless you align your reality with the divine reality."

of us who have heavenly glory not seek darkness, which is the body and the house of bondage. Do not be unfaithful but faithful, and forgive one another. Look, I have been hanging for six days and I have received the rebuke of the trustworthy Christ, because I returned nothing but evil to you and placed stumbling blocks before my righteousness. And now I am going up to the heights. Therefore do not be gloomy but rather be glad and rejoice greatly, because I am leaving behind this dwelling place, that is to say, my body, escaping the corruption of the dragon, which punishes every soul living in sins."

35. After looking around at the crowds, Philip said: "O You who have come up from the dead, from Hades and the swallowing of the abyss, and a luminous cross led you up to the surface[75] because of the goodness of the Father and the Son and the Holy Spirit.[76] This one, being God, became a man, having become incarnate by means of the virgin Mary; remaining immortal in the flesh even after he entered into death, he raised the dead, having mercy on the human race, destroying the sting of sin. He was great but became small for our sake, until he might make the small grow and bring them into his greatness. He is the one who possesses tenderness, and they spit upon him and gave him gall to drink, so that he might make those who had become embittered taste his tenderness. Therefore cleave to him and do not forsake him, for he is our life forever."

36. When Philip completed this proclamation, he said to them: "Release Bartholomew." And they approached and released him. Then Philip said to him: "Bartholomew, my brother in the Lord, you know that the Lord sent you with me into this city, and you have shared with me in all the dangers with our sister Mariamne. But understand that your exit from the body is ordained to happen in Lycaonia, and it has been allotted to Mariamne to go out from her body in the Jordan River. Now, then, I command you both that when I go out from my body you build a church on this spot in which I depart from the body. And with respect to the leopard and the goat's kid, allow them into the church as a sign for those who believe; and let Nicanora care for them, until they depart from the body. And when they depart, bury them close to the

---

[75] Though ὕψος normally means "height," the context here demands "surface," i.e., the top of the abyss.

[76] The Trinitarian formula found in *Vaticanus graecus 824* (V) marks it as more orthodox than *Xenophontos 32* (A), which refers only to Christ.

porch of the church. Place your peace on the house of Stachys, just as that one has placed his peace on this city.

"Let all of the virgins who have believed stay in that house, each day visiting those who are sick, proceeding two by two; but let them not associate with young men, lest Satan tempt them. For the serpent creeps along and through Eve made Adam to slip into death. So it will not happen again in this time as it did in the time of Eve.[77] For it will be a time and a season of evil, and many will be immersed only in the word in that time, but not in its power, living celibately with respect to their bodily members yet fornicating in their hearts. The fornication of their eyes will increase like the Flood. They will increase their attention to specious pleasures, neglecting the knowledge of the gospel, their hearts swelling with arrogance, eating and drinking in Christ during their worship, though neglecting the holy commandment and nullifying it. That generation will be perverted, but blessed is the one who withdraws into his inner chambers, for he will find rest at his departure.

"Do you not know, Bartholomew, that the word of our Lord is true life and knowledge? For our Lord while teaching us said: 'Whoever gazes at a woman and desires her in his heart has committed adultery.' For this reason our brother Peter fled from every place in which a woman was present. But he was still in danger of falling into scandal over his own daughter. And he prayed to the Lord and she was paralyzed on her side so that she might not be deceived. You see, brother, that sight brings evil speech and is the beginning of sin, just as it is written: 'When Eve looked, she saw the tree, that it was pleasing to her eyes and good to eat'; and she was deceived. So let the hearing of the virgins be holy. And in their going out let them proceed together, two by two, because many are the ways of the enemy. Let their gait and manner be in good order, so that they might be saved. Otherwise their fruit will be in vain.[78]

37. "As for you, Bartholomew, be a good overseer;[79] and you will give these instructions to Stachys and will appoint him bishop. But do not entrust the office of bishop to a young man, lest the gospel of Christ be put to shame. Let everyone who teaches possess deeds that match their words.

---

[77] The following text down to the end of section 36 is lacking in *Vaticanus graecus 824* (V) and is taken from *Xenophontos 32* (A).

[78] This is the end of the section found in *Xenophontos 32* (A); we return to *Vaticanus graecus 824* (V).

[79] The term here is δοκιμαστής, "scrutinizer," "approver," "discriminator."

"Now as for me, I am going to the Lord. Take my body and prepare it for burial in leaves of Syrian paper. And do not place a linen shroud on me, because the body of the Lord was wrapped up in linen cloth. When my body has been prepared for burial in the paper leaves, bind it with papyrus cords and bury it in the church. Be at prayer for me, all of you, for forty days, that the Lord might forgive my transgression which I committed when I repaid those who did evil to me. Listen, Bartholomew, where my blood drips on the ground a plant will rise up and it will become a vine and produce grapes. When you pick a cluster of grapes, squeeze it out into the cup, and after you partake of it on the third day, lift up the amen to heaven so that it may become a perfect offering."

38. After Philip said these things he prayed as follows: "Lord Jesus Christ, Father of the ages, King of light, you who have made us wise by your wisdom and given your intelligence to us. You have granted us your grace and the counsel of your goodness, you who have never been separated from us. You are the one who removes the disease of those who take refuge in you. You are the one who has given us the boldness of your wisdom, the one who has given us signs and wonders and has turned back those who were led astray. You are the one who crowns those who defeat the enemy. You are the good presider and prize giver at the contest. Come now, Jesus, and give me the eternal crown of victory over every hostile power and authority, and let not their dark air overshadow me, that I may pass through the waters of fire and all the abyss. Yes, my Lord Jesus Christ, let not the enemy have a place to accuse me before your tribunal, but clothe me with your glorious robe and bright seal that is always shining until I pass by all the world rulers and the evil dragon that opposes us. Now then, my Lord Jesus Christ, make me worthy to meet you in the air, having forgiven me for the retribution which I visited upon my enemies. Transform the form of my body in angelic glory and give me rest in your bliss, and I will receive what was promised from you, what you promised to your saints, forever, amen."

39. After Philip said these things he gave up his spirit while all the crowds were looking at him and crying. So his life was brought to completion in peace, and everyone called out the amen.

40. Then Bartholomew and Mariamne took down his body and they did as Philip had commanded them and buried him in that place. And a voice came out of heaven: "Philip the apostle has been crowned with the

crown of immortality by the presider of the contest, Jesus Christ." And everyone called out the amen.

41. After three days a grapevine sprouted where the blood of the apostle Philip had dripped. And they did all the things that had been commanded them by him, bringing offerings for forty days and praying constantly. They built a church in that place, having also appointed Stachys as bishop. And Nicanora and all the faithful were gathering and they glorified God without ceasing on account of the wonderful things that had taken place among them. And the entire city believed in the name of Jesus. Bartholomew commanded Stachys to baptize those who had believed in the name of the Father and the Son and the Holy Spirit so that they might say "amen."

42. After the forty days the savior appeared in the form of Philip and said to Bartholomew and Mariamne: "My beloved brothers, do you wish to repose in the rest of God? Paradise has opened to me and I have entered into the glory of God. Depart now also yourselves into the places that have been allotted to you. For the appointed plant has been planted in this city and it will bear fruit well enough." So after they said goodbye to the brothers and sisters and prayed for each of them, they went out from the city of Ophioryme of Hierapolis of Asia. Bartholomew left for Lycaonia, and Mariamne proceeded to the Jordan. But Stachys and those with him remained, holding fast to the church in Christ Jesus our Lord, to whom be glory and power now and always, forever and ever, amen.

BIBLIOGRAPHY

Amsler, Frédéric. *Acta Philippi: Commentarius*. Corpus Christianorum: Series Apocryphorum 12. Turnhout: Brepols, 1999.
———. "Amphiloque d'Iconium, Contre les hérétiques encratites et apotactites. Traduction française." Pages 7-40 in *Études réunies en l'honneur de Jean-Daniel Kaestli et Éric Junod*. Edited by Albert Frey and Remi Gounelle. Publications de l'Institut romand des sciences bibliques 5. Prahins, Switzerland: Zebre, 2007.
———. "The Apostle Philip, the Viper, the Leopard, and the Kid: The Masked Actors of a Religious Conflict in Hierapolis of Phrygia (*Acts of Philip* VII-XV and *Martyrdom*)." Pages 432-37 in *Society of Biblical Literature 1996 Seminar Papers*. SBL Seminar Papers 35. Atlanta: Society of Biblical Literature, 1996.
———. "Les Actes de Philippe. Aperçu d'une compétition religieuse en Phrygie." Pages 125-40 in *Le mystère apocryphe. Introduction à une littérature méconnue*, Essais Bibliques 26. Edited by Jean-Daniel Kaestli and Daniel Marguerat. Geneva: Labor et Fides, 1995.
———. "Remarques sur la réception liturgique et folklorique des *Actes de Philippe* (*APh* VIII-XV et *Martyre*)." *Apocrypha* 8 (1997): 251-64.
Amsler, Frédéric, François Bovon, and Bertrand Bouvier. *Actes de l'apôtre Philippe*. Introduction and notes by Frédéric Amsler; translation by François Bovon, Bertrand Bouvier, and Frédéric Amsler. Apocryphes 8. Turnhout: Brepols, 1996.

———. "Les Actes de Philippe." Pages 1179–1320 in *Écrits apocryphes chrétiens*, I, Bibliothèque de la Pléiade 442. Edited by François Bovon and Pierre Geoltrain. Paris: Gallimard, 1997.

Avner, Rina. "The Account of Caesarea by the Piacenza Pilgrim and the Recent Archaeological Discovery of the Octagonal Church in Caesarea Maritima." *Palestine Exploration Quarterly* 140 (2008): 203–12.

Batiffol, Pierre. "Actus sancti Philippi Apostoli nunc primum edidit R. D. Petrus Batiffol." *Analecta Bollandiana* 9 (1890): 204–49.

Bishop, Eric. "Which Philip?" *Anglican Theological Review* 28 (1946): 154–59.

Blond, Georges. "L'hérésie' encratite vers la fin du quatrième siècle." *Recherche de science religieuse* 32 (1944): 157–210.

Bonis, Constantine. "What Are the Heresies Combatted in the Work of Amphilochios, Metropolitan of Iconium (ca 341/5–ca 395/400) 'Regarding False Asceticism'." *Greek Orthodox Theological Review* 6 (1963): 79–96.

Bovon, François. "The Child and the Beast: Fighting Violence in Ancient Christianity." *Harvard Theological Review* 92 (1999): 369–92.

———. "Editing the Apocryphal Acts of the Apostles." Pages 1–35 in Bovon, Brock, and Matthews, *Apocryphal Acts of the Apostles*.

———. "Facing the Scriptures: Mimesis and Intertextuality in the *Acts of Philip*." Pages 138–53 in *Mimesis and Intertextuality in Antiquity and Christianity*. Studies in Antiquity and Christianity. Edited by Dennis R. MacDonald. Harrisburg, Pa.: Trinity Press International, 2001.

———. "From Vermont to Cyprus: A New Witness of the *Acts of Philip*." *Apocrypha* 20 (2009): 9–27.

———. "La vie des apôtres, traditions bibliques et narrations apocryphes." Pages 141–58 in *Les Actes apocryphes des apôtres. Christianisme et monde païen*. Publications de la Faculté de théologie de l'Université de Genève 4. Edited by François Bovon. Geneva: Labor et Fides, 1981.

———. "Le privilège pascal de Marie-Madeleine." *New Testament Studies* 30 (1984): 50–62.

———. "Les Actes de Philippe." Pages 4431–4527 in *Aufstieg und Niedergang der römischen Welt*, II.25.6. Edited by Wolfgang Haase and Hildegard Temporini. Berlin: de Gruyter, 1988.

———. "Mary Magdalene in the *Acts of Philip*." Pages 75–89 in *Which Mary? The Marys of Early Christian Tradition*. SBL Symposium Series 19. Edited by F. Stanley Jones. Atlanta: Society of Biblical Literature, 2002.

———. "Mary Magdalene's Paschal Privilege." Pages 228–35 in Bovon, *New Testament Traditions and Apocryphal Narratives*. Translated by Jane Haapiseva-Hunter. Allison Park, Pa.: Pickwick, 1995.

———. *New Testament and Christian Apocrypha*. Wissenschaftliche Untersuchungen zum Neuen Testament 237. Tübingen: Mohr Siebeck, 2009.

———. "Philip, Acts of." Page 312 in *The Anchor Bible Dictionary*. Vol. 5. Edited by David N. Freedman. New York: Doubleday, 1992.

———. "Philip, Acts of." Pages 951–52 in *The Cambridge Dictionary of Christianity*. Edited by Daniel Patte. Cambridge: Cambridge University Press, 2010.

———. "Philippos [28]." Cols. 809–10 in *Der Neue Pauly, Enzyklopädie der Antike*. Vol. 9. Edited by H. Cancik and H. Schneider. Stuttgart: Metzler, 2000.

———. *Studies in Early Christianity*. Wissenschaftliche Untersuchungen zum Neuen Testament 161. Tübingen: Mohr Siebeck, 2003.

———. "The Synoptic Gospels and the Noncanonical Acts of the Apostles." *Harvard Theological Review* 81 (1988):19–36.

———. "Women Priestesses in the Apocryphal *Acts of Philip*." Pages 109–21 in *Walk in the Ways of Wisdom: Essays in Honor of Elisabeth Schüssler Fiorenza*. Edited by Shelly Matthews, Cynthia Briggs Kittredge, and Melanie Johnson-Debaufre. Harrisburg, Pa.: Trinity Press International, 2003.

Bovon, François, and Bertrand Bouvier. "Actes de Philippe, I, d'après un manuscrit inédit." Pages 367–94 in *Œcumenica et Patristica. Festschrift für Wilhelm Schneemelcher zum 75. Geburtstag*. Edited by D. Papandreou, W. A. Bienert, and K. Schäferdiek. Stuttgart: W. Kohlhammer, 1989.

Bovon, François, and Pierre Geoltrain, eds. *Écrits apocryphes chrétiens*. Vol. 1. Bibliothèque de la Pléiade 442. Paris: Gallimard, 1997.

Bovon, François, and Éric Junod. "Reading the Apocryphal Acts of Apostles." Pages 161–71 in *The Apocryphal Acts of Apostles*. Semeia 38. Edited by Dennis Ronald MacDonald. Decatur, Ga.: Scholars Press, 1986.

Bovon, François, Bertrand Bouvier, and Frédéric Amsler. *Acta Philippi: Textus.* Corpus Christianorum: Series Apocryphorum 11. Turnhout: Brepols, 1999.

Bovon, François, Ann Graham Brock, and Christopher R. Matthews, eds. *The Apocryphal Acts of the Apostles: Harvard Divinity School Studies.* Religions of the World. Cambridge, Mass.: Harvard University Center for the Study of World Religions, 1999.

Bovon, François, et al. *Les Actes apocryphes des apôtres. Christianisme et monde païen.* Publications de la Faculté de théologie de l'Université de Genève 4. Geneva: Labor et Fides, 1981.

Corssen, P. "Die Töchter des Philippus." *Zeitschrift für die neutestamentliche Wissenschaft* 2 (1901): 289–99.

Erbetta, Mario. *Atti e Leggende.* Gli Apocrifi del Nuovo Testamento 2. Turin: Marietti, 1966.

Flamion, Joseph. "Les trois recensions grecques du Martyre de l'apôtre Philippe." Pages 215–25 in *Mélanges d'histoire offerts à Charles Moeller: à l'occasion de son jubilé de 50 années de professorat à l'Université de Louvain. 1863–1913.* Vol. 1: *Antiquité et Moyan âge.* Université de Louvain: Recueil de travaux publiés par les membres des conférences d'histoire et de philologie 40. Louvain: Bureau du Recueil, 1914.

Frey, Albert. "L'Éloge de Philippe, saint apôtre et évangéliste du Christ (BHG 1530b)." *Apocrypha* 3 (1992): 165–209.

Geerard, Maurice. *Clavis Apocryphorum Novi Testamenti.* Corpus Christianorum. Turnhout: Brepols, 1992.

Henschen, Godfried, and Daniel von Papenbrœck, eds. "De S. Philippo Apostolo Martyre Hierapoli Phrygia." Pages 7–18, 733–35 in *Acta Sanctorum Maii.* Vol. 1. Antwerp: Michaelis Cnobarum, 1680.

Holl, Karl. "Die Entstehung der vier Fastenzeiten in der griechischen Kirche." In *Abhandlungen der Berliner Akademie der Wissenschaften 1923.* Philosophisch-historische Klasse 5. Repr., Karl Holl, *Gesammelte Aufsätze zur Kirchengeschichte.* Vol. 2, *Der Osten,* 155–203. Tübingen: Mohr Siebeck, 1928.

James, Montague Rhodes. *The Apocryphal New Testament.* Oxford: Clarendon, 1969.

———. "Supplement to the Acts of Philip." Pages 158–63 in *Apocrypha Anecdota.* Texts and Studies 2.3. Edited by Montague Rhodes James. Cambridge: Cambridge University Press, 1893. Repr., Nendeln, Liechtenstein: Kraus, 1967.

Junod, Éric, and Jean-Daniel Kaestli. *L'histoire des Actes apocryphes des apôtres du IIIe au IXe siècle: le cas des Actes de Jean*. Cahiers de la Revue de théologie et de philosophie 7. Lausanne: Revue de théologie et de philosophie, 1992.

Kurfess, Alfons. "Zu den Philippus-Akten." *Zeitschrift für die neutestamentliche Wissenschaft* 44 (1952-1953): 145-51.

Lambert, A. "Apotactites et Apotaxamènes." Cols. 2604-26 in *Dictionnaire d'archéologie chrétienne et de liturgie*. Vol. 1.2. Paris: Letouzey et Ané, 1924.

Leloir, Louis. *Écrits apocryphes sur les apôtres. Traduction de l'édition arménienne de Venise*. Corpus Christianorum: Series Apocryphorum 4. Turnhout: Brepols, 1992.

Le Nain de Tillemont, Louis-Sébastien. *Mémoires pour servir à l'histoire ecclésiastique des six premiers siècles*. . . . Vol. 1. 2d ed. Paris: Robustel, 1701.

Lipsius, Richard Adelbert. *Die apokryphen Apostelgeschichten und Apostellegenden. Ein Beitrag zur altchristlichen Literaturgeschichte*. II.2 and *Eränzungsband*. Braunschweig: Schwetschke, 1884. Repr., Amsterdam: Philo, 1976.

———. "Zu den Acten des Philippus." *Jahrbücher für protestantische Theologie* 17 (1891): 459-73.

Lipsius, Richard Adelbert, and Maximilien Bonnet. *Acta Apostolorum Apocrypha*. Vol. 2.2. Leipzig: Mendelssohn, 1903. Repr., Darmstadt: Wissenschaftliche Buchgesellschaft, 1959.

Matthews, Christopher R. "Articulate Animals: A Multivalent Motif in the Apocryphal Acts of the Apostles." Pages 205-32 in Bovon, Brock and Matthews, *Apocryphal Acts of the Apostles*.

———. *Philip: Apostle and Evangelist. Configurations of a Tradition*. Supplements to Novum Testamentum 105. Leiden: Brill, 2002.

Molinari, Andrea Lorenzo. "Petrine Traditions in the *Acts of Philip: Letter of Peter to Philip*, a Variant of a Q Saying Found in Matthew 18:21-22, *Acts of Peter* and the *Acts of Peter and the Twelve Apostles*." Pages 1-23 in *Society of Biblical Literature 2000 Seminar Papers 39*. Atlanta: Society of Biblical Literature, 2000.

Noret, Jacques. "Fragments palimpsestes en onciales d'un ménologe de Novembre." *Analecta Bollandiana* 92 (1974): 386.

Peres, A., ed. *Hierapolis di Frigia 1957-1987*. Politecnico di Torino, Università di Lecce, Sezione Archeologica, Istituto Italiano di Cultura di Ankara. Milan: Fabbri, 1987.

Peterson, Erik. "Die Begegnung mit dem Ungeheuer: Hermas, Visio IV." *Vigiliae Christianae* 8 (1954): 52–71.

———. "Die Häretiker der Philippus-Akten." *Zeitschrift für die neutestamentliche Wissenschaft* 31 (1932): 97–111.

———. "Die Philippus-Akten im armenischen Synaxar." *Theologische Quartalschrift* 113 (1933): 289–98.

———. "Zum Messalianismus der Philippus-Akten." *Oriens Christianus* (3d series) 7 (1932): 172–79.

Santos Otero, Aurelio de. "Jüngere Apostelakten." Pages 424–32 in *Neutestamentliche Apokryphen in deutscher Übersetzung* 5. Auflage der von Edgar Hennecke begründeten Sammlung, II. Edited by Wilhelm Schneemelcher. Tübingen: Mohr Siebeck, 1989.

Slater, Richard N. "An Inquiry into the Relationship between Community and Text: The Apocryphal *Acts of Philip* I and the Encratites of Asia Minor." Pages 281–306 in Bovon, Brock, and Matthews, *Apocryphal Acts of the Apostles*.

Stölten, H. O. "Zur Philippuslegende: Bemerkungen." *Jahrbücher für protestantische Theologie* 17 (1891): 149–60.

Thilo, Johann Karl. *Acta S. Thomae apostoli*. Leipzig: Vogel, 1823.

Tischendorf, Constantin. *Acta apostolorum apocrypha*. . . . Leipzig: Avenarius et Mendelssohn, 1851.

———. *Apocalypses apocryphae*. . . . Leipzig: Mendelssohn, 1866. Repr., Hildesheim: Olms, 1966.

van Esbroeck, Michel. *Les plus anciens homéliaires géorgiens. Étude descriptive et historique*. Publications de l'Institut Orientaliste de Louvain 10. Louvain-la-Neuve: Université Catholique de Louvain, Institut Orientaliste, 1975.

Walker, Alexander. "Of the Journeyings of Philip the Apostle. From the Fifteenth Act until the End, and among Them the Martyrdom." Pages 497–503 in *The Ante-Nicene Fathers: Translations of the Writings of the Fathers down to A.D. 325*. Vol. 8. Edited by A. Roberts and J. Donaldson. Edinburgh, 1895. Repr., Peabody, Mass.: Hendrickson, 1994.

www.ingramcontent.com/pod-product-compliance
Lightning Source LLC
Chambersburg PA
CBHW030345240426
43661CB00052B/1750